THE NAME DROPPER

OR

"PEOPLE I SCHLEPPED* WITH"

*(verb: to bring,
to take, to do with)*

BY MORRIS I. DIAMOND

THE NAME DROPPER OR "PEOPLE I SCHLEPPED WITH"
©2011 MORRIS I. DIAMOND

Published in the USA by:

BEARMANOR MEDIA
P.O. BOX 71426
ALBANY, GEORGIA 31708
www.BearManorMedia.com

ISBN-10: 1-59393-653-2 (alk. paper)
ISBN-13: 978-1-59393-653-2 (alk. paper)

BOOK DESIGN AND LAYOUT BY VALERIE THOMPSON.

TABLE OF CONTENTS

DEDICATION PAGE

These are the people that nudged me, hocked me, and hit me over the head until I settled down to write this book I owe them a world of "Thanks."

MY DAUGHTERS—JOANNE MASTERSON AND
ALLYN MARIE GEINOSKY

ALICE HARNELL

ELENA DIAMOND

BILL MARX

A percentage of proceeds netted from the sale of this book will be donated to:

ONJCWC—Olivia Newton-John Cancer Wellness Center
THE CITY OF HOPE
The Montage Initiative, Inc.
(Women's rights in India)

INTRODUCTION

As is done in all acceptance speeches, whether it be for an Oscar, a Grammy, a Tony or an Irving, or whatever, it is inevitable that a cliché will be thrown in by the honoree suggesting that "of all the people I have to thank, I just know that I'm going to unintentionally leave someone out...but you know who you are, and you know I do love you."

Well, in the game of Name Dropping, it is impossible for me to remember every person or incident of notoriety that has touched my life; and if, in the course of breezing through my life, I have omitted someone...well, you know who you are, and you know that I love you for being a part of my life.

I'm not terribly thrilled at the thought of making this an autobiographical epic. After all, who really is all that excited about this life of mine? I can just see it now—movie marquees blaring—Sergeant York; Emile Zola; Louis Pasteur; Ben-hur; Morris I. Diamond?—nope, it just doesn't work; not in my life.

However, it was fate that I ended up in the music business at an early age, and that enabled me to grow with those I became associated with. The ability to grasp the friendships of notables early in their careers and stay close with them through the years gave me the confidence that, whether it be my next door neighbor or an actor with a number one series on television, I found that I could deal with them on a one to one basis and form a friendship that could go beyond the boundaries of just a business or passing relationship.

I also found that by being a confidant to a person of notoriety can only be achieved when you can prove that you are not after the obvious. In due time, the obvious will come in the form of mutual admiration.

My stories are not an addendum to *How to Make Friends and Influence People*...not by a long shot...I am not the one to preach the gospel and tell someone how to make friends. That is something you have to feel for yourself. There has to be a chemistry, a charisma, a mutual admiration society-type of meeting of the minds. Friendship does not have to be a love-at-first-sight application. It can develop, and, like wine, the older it gets...yes, you guessed it.

I don't know if I have set any kind of stage as to what to expect in the following pages, but you should, at this point, have some sort of a reading as to where my head is at. I will try to make this as un-biographical as is possible. All I want to do is tell the world about personalities and humans as well, that have touched my life and my experiences with them.

Look at it this way...in the course of making this an interesting project for you to keep between your bookends; I want to be your very own personal Name Dropper.

Chapter One
TOMMY DORSEY—
THE BEGINNING

In the late '30s, while attending Theodore Roosevelt High School in The Bronx, I served as Entertainment Editor, and at times, Sports Editor. It was during my term as Entertainment Editor that our teacher/advisor received an invitation from The Hotel New Yorker in Manhattan to have a student member of the high school newspaper attend a luncheon and show featuring Tommy Dorsey and his orchestra, to be followed by an interview session. I was selected to attend along with reps from other high schools and colleges in and around the New York area.

I brought my friend, Ben Wertheimer. I liked him because his father was a cop...but Ben was good company and he lived near me in The Bronx, but didn't go to Roosevelt High.

The luncheon was delightful as was the music of Tommy Dorsey. I was always a huge fan of good music, listening to the remote broadcasts from the different hotels around the country every night before going into dreamland.

After lunch, all attendees were herded into a small ballroom where we had a chance to go one-on-one with Mr. Dorsey. I would guess there were about 50 or 60 of us from different high schools and colleges.

Tommy was his charming best and delightful and easy to chat with. I had an idea! I raised my hand to ask why he doesn't start a fan club of high school reporters everywhere he plays around the country. At which point, he yelled out for Jack Egan, his PR rep, to get my name and contact info. They both loved the idea.

In subsequent bookings in the New York area, I would be called by Jack Egan to be their guest. Finally, within a year, we put the

Gathering of high school reporters. Tommy Dorsey and me (18 yrs old) standing at the right.

national fan club of high school reporters into motion. We decided to call our group "The Scribes of Sentimental Swing"; mainly because Tommy was always introduced as "The Sentimental Gentleman of Swing." We put out a weekly newspaper that was sent to anyone that listened to Martin Block's "The Make Believe Ballroom" on WNEW and requested a copy. We also had club pins made which was blue and gold with a trombone crossing a quill pen. Tommy paid all the expenses. In years to follow, he would introduce me as the big mouth that cost him $50,000…all in jest— I think!

I graduated high school in late 1939 and took a job as a book-keeper/secretary at the Fulton Fish Market. I had to be at work by 4 a.m. every morning. After a few months of that I couldn't take the early morning odors of the fish market and I quit the job.

About a month later, Tommy Dorsey and Orchestra opened at The Paramount Theatre. I went down to pay him a visit on the 2nd

The bulk of the Tommy Dorsey band. In the back are the Pied Pipers, Jo Stafford, Frank Sinatra and Buddy Rich. Center row, Ziggy Elman on trumpet. Connie Haines in front.

day of his appearance. He and his manager, Bobby Burns, sat me down to tell me that their band boy, Frank Shaw, was driving their instrument truck back to New York from California where they just finished shooting a movie and would I be interested in working with them backstage at The Paramount running errands for everyone, including the band members until the band boy returned. They assured me that the job would be at least until the end of the three weeks engagement at The Paramount. I didn't hesitate a second and accepted the offer. I think I was getting $10 a week from Mr. Burns' expense account, but I made much more running errands for the guys in the band, who were generous in their tipping.

Shortly before the end of the engagement, Frank Shaw showed up. At that point, I was offered a permanent job as Frank's assistant. Now I'm on the payroll and making $16 weekly as assistant band boy. Plus, Ziggy Elman, the great trumpeter, said he'd pay me $5 per week just to take care of his fan mail and sign his name to photos. He was very popular.

The band taking a pee break on the road—Tommy Dorsey chatting with manager Leonard Vannerson.

I spent the next few months traveling with the band. I was told that I'd have to room with Buddy Rich. I had wondered why he didn't (or wouldn't) room with one of his band mates, but I found no problem with Buddy at all. He never had any money...he would always borrow a dollar or two while on the road, but when we returned to New York, his father was always at the depot or station and would immediately repay me for his son's debts.

I rather enjoyed setting up and tearing down the bandstand, schlepping instruments to and from the bus or train. If we were within driving distance of New York City, we would take the bus...or the band and Tommy would take the bus while Frank and I drove the van with Tommy's instruments and his personal trunks.

On my very first road trip after the Paramount, Frank and I drove the van up to New England. When we got there and began to unload, we noticed that one of Tommy's wardrobe trunks landed on his favorite trombone while in transit. Well, he always had a few more trombones along and we figured that we'd set up the bandstand and put another of his trombones on the stage.

Everything was all set up beautifully...until Tommy stepped in front of the band, picked up his horn to play his theme song, "I'm Getting Sentimental Over You"...then all hell broke loose. He threw the horn down and in front of the crowd, fired us. We did find another horn that pleased him.

During the intermission, he called us into his dressing room and had cooled down considerably. He wanted to know what had happened to his horn, and all we could do was tell him the truth...that one of his trunks fell on the horn while in transit. He accepted that and told us we're not fired and that on the way back to New York City, we should drop the trombone off at the factory in Hartford for them to repair. Which we did and the factory had Tommy's horn back in a few days and all went well.

After being with the band for about six months, for whatever reason, Tommy dismissed Bobby Burns, his manager, and he hired Benny Goodman's ex-manager, Leonard Vannerson. He was also married to Martha Tilton, Benny Goodman's vocalist.

The second day Leonard was on the job, he called me in and mentioned that he doesn't see the sense of two band boys, and I knew for sure this was it, I'm being fired. But instead he asked if I could type. I replied that I took a commercial course in high school and yes, I could type and also do shorthand.

He immediately made me his right hand with the title of assistant manager. At the end of the first week he asked me to do the payroll. I told him that I never did accounting; I wouldn't know what to do. He showed me the ledger and told me to do the same this week that he did last week. Just make out the checks for everyone and keep the balance correct in the ledger.

One day I was doing the payroll on the road and Frank Sinatra came in to my hotel room while I was writing payroll checks and wanted to know how much Buddy Rich was making. I covered the ledger with my body and said I can't do that. He said, "C'mon,

L-R Pianist Joe Bushkin, Me, Leonard Vennerson, Frank Sinatra—another pee break.

Moishe, I won't tell anyone." I still wouldn't tell him...that he and Buddy were making the same $125 weekly.

Tommy treated me like his son. He would yell at me when he saw me at a bar with the "likes" of Frank Sinatra or Don Lodice. He offered to buy me books on management so I could study and some day be capable of managing an artist.

I stayed with the band until I was called into service in August, 1942. Sinatra had left the band about a month earlier.

Ken Curtis who sang with Shep Fields was waiting for the call to replace Frank, but unfortunately, he was drafted into the army before that could happen. Also in the bullpen waiting for his turn to sing with the band was Dick Haymes. It was my birthday about that time, and all the guys gave me little gifts. Ziggy gave me a beautiful tie clip and cuff links with musical notes on them... Dick Haymes gave me a pair of white socks!! Well, they did fit!

I was discharged from the Air Transport Command of the US Air Force on April 12, 1945; the day that President Roosevelt died. I always liked to think that he was so upset and heartbroken at me leaving the service that he just couldn't take it and passed away. Then reality set in.

When I was discharged, I was at the air base in Long Beach, California. I visited my sister in Burbank before I left for home back East. While in Burbank, I hailed a taxi and asked if he knew where Frank Sinatra's home was in Toluca Lake. He did. At this time Frank was doing well with a new radio show on NBC.

I took the cab and had him wait outside Frank's home not knowing if he'd be there or if he'd even want to see me. All went well. I was welcomed with open arms by Frank and Nancy.

A letter from Jo Stafford.

We chatted for a while. Frank offered to phone George Evans, his press agent and have him hire me to work exclusively on Frank. That would have been my first job offer getting back to civilian life. I told Frank that I'd like to get back home first and visit with my parents before I make any decision. He gave me his phone number to call when I made up my mind and had Ritchie Lisella, one-time band boy with the early Dorsey band, drive me back to my sister's home in Burbank.

Now back in New York, I visited my parents in The Bronx and all went well. I then took the subway to Manhattan and paid a visit to the Dorsey office which was the Penthouse on top of the Brill Building, 1619 Broadway. Most of the occupants of the building were major music publishing companies. It also housed two famous restaurants, Jack Dempsey's and The Turf. That was also the offices of the music publishing companies owned by Tommy. Embassy Music and Dorsey Brothers Music, managed by Jack Johnstone.

By sheer coincidence, Tommy Dorsey happened to be in his office when I arrived and was greeted warmly. He offered me a job as road manager of the band. I thanked him but declined only because of three years of army life, I had my fill of traveling and wanted to settle down.

At that point, Tommy had to leave for an engagement in Buffalo and was being taken to the train by Jack Johnstone, and Tommy suggested I wait until Jack returns to have further conversation with me. I agreed.

Jack arrived back at his office about forty minutes later and we chatted. He told me that Tommy would like to have me as part of the organization and would I like to be a song plugger.

I had always admired the song pluggers when they'd pitch their songs to Tommy while traveling with the band. I accepted the job. I liked that idea and the offer was generous.

I performed my job as a song plugger much better than I thought I could. I was able to get our songs to singers who once were in Dorsey's favor, but for whatever reason, their friendships with him dissipated over the years. One instance in particular were Jo Stafford and the Pied Pipers, who, when they left Dorsey to go out on their own, caused resentment from their boss because he thought he had them for the rest of their lives. The Pipers were able to get a recording contract, along with a separate recording contract for Jo Stafford and her husband, Paul Weston. Paul was one of the ever present arrangers for the Dorsey band along with Axel Stordahl and Sy Oliver. When he arranged for Dorsey, Paul Weston went under the name of Paul Wetstein, which I surmise, was his real name.

They also had a weekly radio show on NBC in 1945 when I started to work as a song plugger. Not having seen them since I went in the Air Force in August, 1942, I wasn't quite sure how I would be received, particularly due to the fact I was once again in the employ of Tommy Dorsey. Boy was I wrong.

I walked into their rehearsal in the studio on the 8th floor at NBC and was greeted like a long lost brother. Hugs and kisses from Jo and the Pipers alleviated my fears and they gladly wanted to help me in my first civilian job and did so by using one of our songs that we published every week for the next couple of months.

That in itself gave me the confidence to go into the world of radio and getting the songs aired that the company I represented published.

The same with Sinatra when he came to New York to play the Paramount Theater. I visited him backstage and again thanked him for offering to call his press agent. He was gracious and bade me good luck on my new job. He later recorded a couple of songs that I was working on.

Thomas Francis Dorsey, Jr. died at the age of 51 on November 26, 1956. He was THE Fabulous Dorsey.

Chapter Two
ZIGGY ELMAN

When I first joined the Dorsey band at The Paramount Theatre in 1941, Harry Aaron Finkelman, a.k.a. Ziggy Elman, was one of the first of the musicians to embrace my arrival. When he found out that, initially, I'll be working with them for three weeks which was the length of their engagement at the theatre; and being paid a very meager salary plus tips, he asked me to take care of his fan mail and he paid me five bucks a week.

Now I was making big bucks! I would've worked for nothing...he was one of my favorite musicians during his tenure with Benny Goodman...not only did he perform the great trumpet solo on "The Angels Sing," but he also wrote the song with a great lyric by Johnny Mercer. Tommy Dorsey had Ziggy perform that tune in every show. For me, that was a super-perk.

Some months later, the band was booked at the fashionable Virginia Beach Hotel. (Today all hotels in Virginia Beach are now named with a brand i.e. Hilton Virginia Beach Hotel, etc.) I figured from the first few minutes of arrival at the hotel that we were going to have a problem when I was bringing Tommy's suitcases along with Ziggy Elman's into the hotel when the manager approached Tommy to advise him that this was a restricted hotel and he couldn't accommodate Mr. Elman with a room. Tommy picked the guy up by his throat and pinned him down against the check-in counter and told him in no uncertain terms that if Ziggy can't stay at the hotel then we would all pull out and would not play there. Tommy was that kind of guy. He loved Ziggy and always made provisions for him to stay in an adjoining suite wherever they played and stayed.

Ziggy Elman and Frank Sinatra at Dorsey's estate in Bernardsville, NJ.

Ziggy had family in Connecticut. He also owned a trombone which he never played while with the band. During one of our breaks while in New York City, he brought me the trombone and asked me to deliver it to his sister in Connecticut if and when I had planned a trip in that direction. I must have held on to that trombone for about three months before I had the opportunity to schlep to Connecticut and make the delivery. But during those three months, I had a chance to acquaint myself with the hows and whys of a trombone. Every time I came home to my apartment, I picked up the horn and tried to play…actually, I had a pretty good ear for music. I could sit down at a piano and was able to one-finger my way through a tune that I heard a few minutes earlier…but the trombone, I found, was a different ball game altogether. I sounded like a cow giving birth. I then figured that it was not in my future to take over as leader of the Tommy Dorsey Orchestra.

Chapter Three
SINATRA—XMAS SONG

As was often the case, Telly Savalas always looked for a reason to take a weekend in Vegas. In the late '60s, his oldest daughter Christina, visiting from back East, was returning to college in Boston.

Aha…a reason to go to Vegas—his eldest daughter's last fling before returning to school.

So off we went; my wife Elena and I and his then wife Lynn and daughter, Christina. We always drove…but only Telly would drive…when he was in a car, no one could give a trip that professional touch as he. He always envisioned himself as the epitome of drivers. I've been in his company when we were limo'd somewhere and he would take over the steering. Imagine pulling up to a red carpet at a premier and everyone's anxious to see who is exiting the limo…and to their surprise, there's Telly getting out on the driver's side.

Anyway, we arrived at Caesar's Palace, checked in and started making plans for the evening. We saw that Sinatra was at the Sands Hotel but we had no reservations for the show, and this was on a Saturday. Telly told us to get ready; that we would go to the Sands Hotel and when they see him playing blackjack, the pit bosses will surely comp him and his party to see the show. Judging from past incidents, he was usually right.

There were five of us, and true to Telly's prediction, after a few minutes of blackjack, he was invited in for the show…but only a table for four…not five. My wife insisted that I go with them and she'll kill time in the casino, which I refused. The three Savalases went in.

Ziggy, Sinatra and me at the Dorsey Estate.

Now I started doing some tall thinking as to how to I get in to see the show...I picked up the house phone and called Buddy Rich (his band was backing Frank). Buddy told me that his father was in the casino going bananas because he couldn't get him a table for this first show.

I remembered that I had a business card given to me by an old friend, Ken Greengrass, who was Steve & Eydie's manager. I took the card from my wallet and wrote on the back—Dear Phil, (he was the Maitre d of the showroom) anything you can do for my friend Morris Diamond, would be appreciated by me...I signed Ken's name to it and gave it to a security guy who was initially reluctant to pass the card on to Phil, but when he saw it was Ken's card he accommodated me. Phil called me over and asked if I was a close friend of Ken's...I told him I was, and also a friend to Steve & Eydie. He had one of his captains direct me and my wife to a table for two. Winding our way thru the showroom, Telly spotted us and wanted to know where we're going because we were heading further towards front than where he was sitting. My wife and I ended up sitting stage right...I mean that my toes were actually touching the stage.

When Frank entered from stage left to perform, he couldn't help but notice us sitting there and did so with an acknowledging nod.

A couple of weeks before this journey, I heard a Christmas song, "Christmas Long Ago," written by TV comedy writer and producer, Sam Denoff. We had been friends since the days when I was a young record promoter and he was writing copy for WNEW radio in NYC. I loved it and they asked me to publish it. I had a singer friend, Burt Taylor, record a demo of it and I took this demo with me to Vegas. I had heard that Frank was getting ready to record a Christmas album and hopefully I would get a chance to get it to him. That chance didn't present itself, so I left the demo and a lyric sheet at the front desk of The Sands the next morning before we left to return to L.A. I also enclosed a little note explaining that I was the publisher of the tune, and leave the rest up to fate as to whether he'll actually get the demo or not.

One week later, also on a Saturday, we got another call from Lynn Savalas asking if we want to go to Nicky Blair's Stefaninos restaurant for dinner on Sunset Boulevard at the beginning of Beverly Hills. Anyway, we set a time for 8 o'clock.

My wife and I arrived at the restaurant a few minutes before 8 p.m. and Nicky did the greeting and seating. Five minutes later, Nicky came over to us to ask if we wouldn't mind sitting at the next table.

Sinatra and me on the patio of the penthouse offices of the Dorsey organization atop the Brill Building in NYC.

The Savalas' and his daughter Christina hadn't arrived as yet. Nicky explained that he just got a call from Sinatra from his plane to tell him he's on his way to L.A. and have dinner at the restaurant with a couple of friends. I thought that was odd because I knew that Frank was still appearing at The Sands Hotel in Vegas and didn't close until the next night. Nick agreed with my thought, shrugged his shoulders and came back with one of his famous lines…"What can I tell you?"

Mildred Fox (her husband took the photo), Sinatra and Sgt. Morris Diamond taking a break on the roof of the Paramount Theatre between shows.

The Savalas' finally arrived, followed by power-agent, George "Bullets" Durgom, who, after greeting us all, told us that he also got a call from Frank ordering him to join him for dinner.

Now, enters the King. His Highness, Frank, along with Jilly and a couple of other friends. Frank was his usual cordial self with a warm handshake for Telly and me and a kiss for the ladies. That was it.

We finished our meals, and waved our goodbyes to the next table, still wondering why he was in LA when he was supposed to be working the Sands in Vegas.

The next day, mind you, this is one week after we returned home from Las Vegas; I had a battery problem with my car and decided to go to the gas station on the corner of LaBrea and Hollywood Boulevard to have it attended to. Of all people, Bullets Durgom pulled into the gas station for a fill-up. He then told me that after I left the restaurant the night before, Frank had mentioned that he saw me in Vegas and in L.A. and did not know I was living in L.A. Bullets mentioned to him that we see each other quite often and knew for a fact that I've been in L.A. for a number of months.

Frank then told Bullets that "Moishe was at The Sands last week and he left me a demo of a Christmas song that I truly liked and will record it in my upcoming Christmas album."

This was Sunday evening. I was walking on cloud nine, ten and eleven. I immediately returned home and called Sam Denoff to tell him the good news…and good news it was…UNTIL…

The next day I got a call from Bullets and he told me the entire story as to why Frank did not work on the evening we all dined together at Nicky Blair's.

It seems that Frank wanted to do a little gambling, and got into a huge argument with the brass at The Sands because they wanted him to get ready for his Saturday night shows. That's when Frank blew a fuse and flew to L.A. for his dinner neglecting the huge Saturday night crowds that amassed outside of the showroom.

When he returned back to the Sands after his L.A. dinner, the matter of his gambling got hot and heavy.

He had asked The Sands' VP, Carl Cohen, to okay a marker for $100,000 and Carl refused. Words got into pushing and pushing got into heavy duty hitting and hitting got into Frank losing a few teeth. Right in the casino.

End result—Frank cancelled his two record sessions. One being an LP with Ella Fitzgerald of songs they had recently performed together on a TV show and the other cancellation was his Christmas album. I had always felt that if Frank ever recorded my song, it would have turned out to be a standard for many years. I know every composer and music publisher feels that way about the tunes they get recorded, but this one had that special feel about it that assured longevity.

A few months later, Telly and I were back in Vegas again for a weekend and Frank was back at work. We went to see his show and, as always, Frank graciously acknowledged Telly's presence to the audience. A few minutes later, Frank's right hand man, Jilly, came to our table to tell us that Frank would like us to join him and few of his buddies at the bar after the show. Which we did. Frank was in a fantastic mood, kibitzing with all of us. He pointed his finger at me and told Telly and the rest of his cronies, "If it wasn't for this putz, I'd be at the Lincoln Hotel on Eighth Avenue in New York, singing with the Jan Garber Orchestra."

In our earlier days when with the Tommy Dorsey Orchestra, I used to get on Frank's case and bug him a lot about thinking of going on his own. There's no question in my mind that it wasn't really my pushing him that made him to finally decide to go out on his own…but it's nice to know that he thought about it years later. Telly was proud of me.

Chapter Four
BUDDY RICH

If you were to ask Louie Bellson or Gene Krupa "Who was the greatest drummer ever?" Hands down they would tell you it was Buddy Rich. I couldn't agree more.

Buddy kept to himself most of the time. When Sinatra would be hanging out with tenor man Don Lodice and a few of the other musicians, Buddy wanted no part of that and spent much of his time with his face in a book.

He never carried any money with him. Here he was making a very good salary of $125 per week, and when we were on the road he would borrow money from me and I was making a huge $16 per week, plus tips. "Hey Moishe, lend me $2, I wanna get a new tie." At the end of every road trip, whether we were on a train, bus or plane, Buddy's father, Robert, would be at the gate and the first thing he would do is reimburse me for the couple of dollar loans that I had given Buddy. His father never asked me for an accounting…he just asked "What do I owe you?" and fork over the few bucks.

To say that Buddy was a very sensitive person would be an understatement. The band was booked at the fashionable Virginia Beach Hotel. The rest of us had rooms at a nearby motel on the beach, including Buddy, who, during the opening show that night, found himself the victim of the anti-Semites on the beach.

That evening the band was set to play and during the first set some hoodlums were hanging out behind the bandstand and started giving Buddy Rich a hard time shouting racial slurs, "Hey, Jew-boy, how does it feel to be with real people?" and "Hey, Jew-boy, why don't you go back to New York with the rest of the Jews?" You could see Buddy fuming. He waited until the end of the set and took after

Buddy Rich and I in the rear and Pied Piper Chuck Lowery taking a break between shows in Buffalo, NY.

them. We couldn't find him. We notified the local police and they located him the next day sitting on a curb a mile down the beach. To say he was upset would be an understatement, but a long chat with Tommy calmed him down and the rest of the week's engagement went without any problems which was assisted by a couple of security personnel in the band area.

There was a lot of talk about the fights between Buddy and Sinatra. The only altercations that I witnessed were more conversational than actual fist fights. Most of the time the "talks" were about Buddy lifting the tempo a bit on Frank's vocals. But Buddy would hear from Mr. Dorsey about that as well.

Little known is that when Buddy, in his later years, had to go to Dr. DeBakey, the famous heart surgeon for consultation and ultimately, surgery, Sinatra had his private plane fly Buddy to Houston. When Buddy passed away in 1987 at the age of 70, again, Frank came through with a beautiful eulogy at the funeral. What is common knowledge is that when Buddy decided to go out on his own with his very own band, Sinatra financed the entire move.

Through the years, Buddy would have a band, then just a trio, then a band again or when things got real bad…he just took jobs playing with different bands and the Jazz at the Philharmonic group.

I regret not having been in touch that much with Buddy through the years, but the fond memories linger on.

Chapter Five
THE BRILL BUILDING AND SINATRA

I would be remiss if I neglected to include this chapter of a momentous occasion that occurred at the new Tommy Dorsey offices in the penthouse atop the Brill Building.

This was during my early 1941/42 years with Tommy working as band boy for the orchestra. He combined his orchestral business offices with his newly acquired music publishing companies, Embassy, Dorsey Brothers and Sun Music.

To document this occasion, Tommy and the manager of the publishing companies, Jack Johnstone, decided to throw a wing-ding of a "new home" party on the premises. The office space covered the entire penthouse, alongside two huge patios on either side, giving a visitor magnificent North and South views of Manhattan. Everybody who was anybody showed up. Drinks and Hors d'oeuvres galore.

Everyone that attended was having a great time...until an incident occurred involving a John Griffith, representing the *New York Enquirer*, who, single-handed, turned a big portion of the festive evening into a big mess.

Obviously, Mr. Griffith had one too many drinks. He walked over to Edythe Wright, ex vocalist with the Dorsey band, and loudly expressed his displeasure at her chatting with "Jew-boy," Harry Goodman (Benny's brother).

Within earshot of the remark was Frank Sinatra, who, without batting an eyelash, took a swing at Griffith who went down like a ton of bricks. Frank then commanded those of us that were near, to help get rid of "this bum." Frank, Hank Sanicola, (a song plugger/ pianist who rehearsed Frank on all tunes given to him by Dorsey

The Dorsey party. In dark glasses, Henry Nemo—the hipster of the music industry who wrote "I Let A Song Go Out of My Heart" with Duke Ellington plus more.

and soon to become Frank's personal manager); Nick Sevano (a friend of Frank's) and myself each took an arm and a leg—dragged Griffith to the elevator, brought him down to the main floor and dragged him further through the long narrow lobby and dumped him on the sidewalk in front of the Brill Building at 1619 Broadway.

There was only one elevator in service that evening, and we asked the lone operator to make sure that he doesn't bring "that guy" back up to the party on the 11th floor.

Sure enough, while the elevator was in service, Griffith walked up the 11 floors to the party. He was spotted and again the four of us performed the same action and dropped him off on Broadway.

Tommy at the time was having his hair cut in his office by his favorite barber, Rudy. He was later informed about the incident and was not happy about it. We were to leave after the party for Penn Station for a gig.

In this photo are the four hoods that carried the *Enquirer's* John Griffith out of the Brill Building. In the front—Sinatra, me. Next row, Nick Sevano. In back, Hank Sanicola, Frank's manager.

As we exited the elevator on the main floor of the Brill Building, there he was—Mr. Griffith—staggering/leaning against the mail drop. Tommy saw red. He walked over to him, grabbed him with one hand—told him in no certain terms what he thought of him, adding, "You're an Irishman and so am I!" and punched him with his other hand.

We all left for the train station, content in our minds that a modicum of justice had been served. Funny thing, there was no mention of the incident in the morning edition of the *New York Enquirer*! Hmmm!

Chapter Six
GEORGE "BULLETS" DURGOM

In 1941, the same time I was band boy for the Tommy Dorsey Orchestra, a gent by the name of "Bullets" Durgom held the same position with the Glen Miller orchestra—as did "Popsie" Randolph, who schlepped instruments for the Benny Goodman Orchestra.

He was nicknamed "Bullets" because of his physical stature. I would dare say that he was easily 5 X 5; a bit chunky, and a huge part in his hair…actually, the part covered his entire scalp (except around the ears).

In early 1942, Tommy Dorsey and his manager, Leonard Vannerson, decided that an advance man was necessary for our tours. They decided that "Bullets," because of his personality, would be perfect. His job would be to go into a city a few days before the band was to perform and set up the press and radio interviews. While he was on the road, I was his liaison in our Brill Building office to coordinate dates and times.

In 1945, while still in the Air Force, I was shipped to the Long Beach airport where, as a flight radio operator, I was assigned to a crew that flew the new B-17s from the Boeing factory on the base and delivered them to flight crews in the US and Canada that would take them to war. I had lost track of "Bullets" during the early years of World War II, and, lo and behold, there he was stationed at the Long Beach Airbase in charge of entertainment.

We connected and spent much time together. He had his car at the base and I would hitch a ride every weekend into Hollywood; go our separate ways, and meet for the return to Long Beach on Sunday nights.

L-R; Al Teller, former head of Columbia Records; the incomparable George "Bullets" Durgom; the inevitable Morris I. Diamond.

We were both discharged from the service about the same time. By the time he opened for business, he already had a few stars under his belt for management. Burgess Meredith was discharged from the service in 1944 and he already had a slew of films under his belt since the mid-30s. He was one of "Bullet's" new clients. Tommy Dorsey vocalist, Connie Haines, was another. After awhile, he worked with Elke Sommer and Jaye P. Morgan. I signed JP to my Beverly Hills Records Company in 1971, thanks to "Bullets," who, along with Telly Savalas and Jack Warner, became investors in my record company. A couple of other TV/Film personalities who "Bullets" guided during their early years were Merv Griffin and Jackie Gleason.

In the '60s while at Mercury Records, I received a call from "Bullets" telling me that he would be coming to Chicago in a couple of weeks with Trini Lopez, who he booked into Mr. Kelly's Night Club for a week. I spent every evening with them during their stay.

I had casually mentioned to him that I've been secretly going to my office at Mercury on weekends and taking a stab at writing scripts for a few of the comedy shows that were currently on TV. He suggested that I stay at it, and in a couple of weeks, send him a few of the scripts...which I did. I mailed him three stories. All original, including one that had the possible makings of a future blockbuster. Well, at least I thought it could be.

He read them through and passed the scripts on to his buddy, Jimmy Komack, who, at the time, was very involved with Jackie Cooper's weekly TV show *Hennessey*. Jimmy phoned me in Chicago and we had a delightful and very encouraging chat. He told me he read the scripts, and although my script structure was not the best, my ideas and dialog were refreshing and felt that I should pursue writing. But he also mentioned that it would be difficult to pitch me to a writing staff while I was still working in Chicago and to phone him should I get the opportunity to get to L.A. in the near future. By sheer coincidence, I had the chance to leave my job at Mercury for a number of reasons, four months later—the least of which was to go to California to be a comedy writer. It just worked out that way and I hit the road to L.A.

As directed by Mr. Komack, I phoned him about two weeks after arriving in L.A. No response. I called for a few days, but in vain. No return call. I wasn't devastated, just disappointed. Fortunately, I had been assigned my first film as music consultant (today known as a Music Supervisor), and time helped me forget about being a comedy writer as more movie and TV music supervising situations came my way. I didn't feel that my situation shouldn't warrant me bugging "Bullets" about it. I never brought it up with him.

We were always in touch through the years either socially or business. In the late '90s, I got a call from "Bullets" asking me if I would like to take a drive to Santa Monica that evening and catch the showcase featuring the daughter of his attorney, Max Fink. I told him that I didn't know that Max Fink's daughter was an entertainer, and that I would love to go see her show. He asked me to pick him up at his apartment that was on Doheny just off Sunset in West L.A. "Ok, see you at seven in front of your building" I answered.

I picked him up as scheduled. He got into my car and said his hello and continued, "Is it ok if we take a ride to Santa Monica and catch Max Fink's daughter who is performing there tonight?" "Bullets" repeated the same question twice more during the twenty minute drive from his apartment. It tore my heart out. That was my first

L-R: "Bullets" Durgom, 2 members of "Rock Bottom," Beverly Hills
Records recording artists, me, the boss of Beverly Hills Records,
and the late Norm Prescott who, along with Lou Scheimer, ran the
Filmation Animation Studios. We all got presents.

knowledge and experience with him that he came down with
Alzheimer's disease. I was thinking to myself that we've known each
other for fifty years and how he looked after me and my record
company to make sure we stayed in business. He did give me Jaye
P. Morgan as one of my recording artists as well as convincing Jack
Warner to invest in my company. He even reached out to Rockford,
Illinois to his brother John to invest in my company.

"Bullets" was a one-of-a-kind person…absolutely irreplaceable as
a friend, and as loveable as my brother. He left us October 24,
1992. A huge void in my life.

Chapter Seven
STUART FOSTER

Stuart was the vocalist with the Tommy Dorsey Orchestra post war. His real name was Tamar Aswad. I managed Stuart in the late fifties to the early sixties. I always claimed that he was one of the best vocalists I had ever heard. He could perform every genre of music—pop or Broadway—to perfection. I couldn't wait to attend his performances and hear him perform "The Soliloquy" from the great Broadway show, *Carousel.* Better than Gordon MacRae, I thought.

He had a good ride in the Galen Drake TV series, along with being featured in a couple of films, *Ever Since Venus* and *The Fabulous Dorseys.* We were also able to get him a record deal with Coral, which he was appreciative of; however, Stuart was thrilled when Gordon Jenkins asked him to record a couple of sides with him on the Decca label. Gordon was the best "string arranger" I had heard.

Stuart's talent paid off when he was signed by super agents, Baum and Newborn. They thought that he was a great talent and booked him everywhere from Vegas to Manhattan. He was married to Pat, one of the Kim-Loo sisters who sang with the Ina Ray Hutton Orchestra.

Stuart was not a tall person—maybe five foot seven—and that was his big frustration that he felt was responsible for his not landing a leading part in a Broadway musical. His passing in 1968 at the age of forty-nine, I felt, was a result of his frustration.

Stuart Foster, Tommy Dorsey vocalist post Sinatra, showing Buddy Rich how to play drums. Yeah!

Recording Artist, Stuart Foster plugging his new recording with Boston DJ, the late Norm Prescott on WORL, Mass.

Chapter Eight
COME ON-A MY HOUSE

As a freelance record promoter in the early '50s, one of my clients was a prominent radio vocalist, Kay Armen. We had moderate success with a few of her previous recordings achieving much airplay and sales. Her manager, Vinnie Andrews, had his own record company and Kay recorded for him. I was his promotion man hired to secure airplay on radio.

He called me in one day to listen to a demo of her latest effort in the studio. The tune was "Come On-a My House," written by Ross Bagdasarian, creator of the Chipmunks. I liked what I heard and asked how soon I could "run" with this new release. He then told me that he spoke with Mitch Miller of Columbia Records and there was a chance that they would release our record nationally if he liked it.

As requested by Mitch, Vinnie messengered the demo over to Columbia Records...this was on a Thursday.

The following Sunday morning, while at home, I was listening to WNEW radio and all of a sudden I hear "Come on-a My House."

But...by Rosemary Clooney. And this was four days after the delivery of Kay's recording to Miller.

Mitch Miller received the demo...liked it...but LOVED the song. He put Rosemary Clooney into the studio that night...and had demos released to the New York City radio stations by Saturday and on the air by Sunday.

Word has it that after Mitch Miller signed Rosemary to Columbia Records, they were at odds because she did not like the material he was picking for her to record. That was the same problem that

Frank Sinatra had during his short stint with Columbia Records. When Mitch heard Kay Armen's record of "Come On-a My-House" he laid the law down and told Rosemary that she either records this song or that's the end of their deal.

If Vinnie Andrews had obtained the publishing rights for this song, then there's no way that Mitch could record it without getting the "mechanical license" from the original music publisher, which in this case, was Ross Bagdasarian's Music Publishing Company. And there's no way in the world that Ross was going to turn down a chance of having a possible hit record with Columbia. Any song is recordable once it has been previously recorded and released, and no permission is necessary. If the record company released the record without obtaining the license, then they would have to pay the music publisher the statutory rate royalties that is in effect at the time of the record being released.

The rest is history!

Chapter Nine
TERRI STEVENS

In 1954 I received a call from Joe Leahy, one of the best arrangers in town at the time. He had just recorded a new singer, Terri Stevens, on a small label, *A* Records. Joe was asked by the owner of the company to seek out an independent record promoter mainly because they had no staff to speak of.

I took the gig.

When I first met Terri, I'm afraid my feelings were obvious. She was gorgeous. A lovely Italian brunette from New Haven. Perfect. Then I also met her husband, Arturo Cano. He owned The Boulevard Nightclub on Queens Boulevard. Everyone played there from Tony Bennett to Don Rickles. This was a natural situation for me. When I had to entertain out of town disc jockeys, we would be very welcome at The Boulevard. Arturo, an envoy from Ecuador, was also credited in bringing to the United States a few well known tennis pros. Not the least of them was Pancho Segura.

Arturo called me one day, Terri was opening for Don Rickles, and he offered a suggestion for a number of disc jockeys and program directors to come in for a dinner and show. I gathered a number of radio personalities and their guests. All was well until Don Rickles went into his routine of picking on someone in the audience. He chose Betty Lazaar and the hat she was wearing, who at the time was married to WNEW's all night DJ, Jack Lazaar. She was incensed and insisted that Jack get up there and punch Don out. Jack tried to explain that this is his routine and to disregard his remarks. End result, Betty walked out and left Jack stranded. I had to schlep him back to Manhattan and WNEW for his midnight show. He was embarrassed.

A fairly recent photo of Terri Stevens, recording and TV artist of the '50s visiting with Celine Dion.

When an artist hires a record promoter, it's generally for six to eight weeks, and then they go off salary until they get a call from the artist to work on the next release. Peggy Lee never took me off payroll for the three years I plugged her records, which was unheard of amongst my peers.

Peggy had an engagement at the Capitol Theatre in Washington, D.C. She phoned me and asked if I would set up some interviews in that city while she was working there, and asked me to come down to Washington and squire her around the city visiting radio stations and doing interviews. That I did and she was very grateful rewarding me with an extra two week bonus.

In 1955, Peggy had a great starring role in the film *Peter Kelly's Blues*, which was produced by Jack Webb, who also starred in the film. At this point, I was not on Peggy's payroll, but I got a call from a very close friend of mine, Herm Saunders, who, for many years, was Jack Webb's right hand man.

He called to ask me if I would take the assignment of working on the soundtrack album from the film. He mentioned the tunes and artists in the soundtrack and I explained to him that I had been Peggy's record promoter and to me, working on the soundtrack would be another labor of love.

And it was. The film did very well and so did the soundtrack sales. Jack Webb and Herm Saunders expressed their thanks and appreciation. That doesn't happen too often.

The last time I saw Peggy was in 1994 when she was the honoree at the Society of Singers annual gala. It bothered me to see her in a wheelchair, but she wore her usual smiling face, and made everyone comfortable that came by her table for a "hello." It was a quick hello and a hug and I was pleased that she remembered a few of the good times we had in the mid-50s. Peggy died January 21, 2004 and her life was celebrated at a Memorial at the Riviera Country Club in Pacific Palisades, California whose audience consisted of the elite of the film, TV and music biz who came to pay their respects. I attended with Jazz Harpist, pianist and vocalist Corky Hale and her song writing husband, Mike Stoller, composer of Peggy's *Is That All There Is?*

Chapter Eleven
MERV GRIFFIN

In the fifties, I was still picking up a client here and there to promote their new recordings on radio, both locally in New York City and nationally as well.

Got a call from Merv Griffin, a one time band singer with Freddy Martin's orchestra, and also, not a well know fact, he was an actor and was responsible for the first open mouthed kiss with Kathryn Grayson in a film called *So This Is Love*. He actually was discovered by Doris Day and she arranged for his getting the role.

Back to the phone call from Merv...He started his own label, Panda Records in 1957 and recorded a song called "I've Got A Lovely Bunch of Coconuts" and asked if I would be interested in promoting his new recording.

I hadn't heard too much about him, but, a buck is a buck and I took on the new client. The record was an instant hit. Not because I promoted it, but it had that lilt to it that appealed to the general public. All I had to do initially was to get the disc jockeys to hear it and once they did, I was home. They all loved it and gave it lots of airtime.

The recording sold quite good, I don't recall the exact amount, but was quickly picked up by record distributors all over the country. The song itself made number one on the Hit Parade and sold over three million copies.

Shortly after that, Merv hosted a Goodson/Todman game show, *Play Your Hunch* which paved the way for other game shows which ultimately led to his own talk show on NBC in 1962.

Needless to say, he had no time to bother with his new record company; consequently there was no follow-up product to work on.

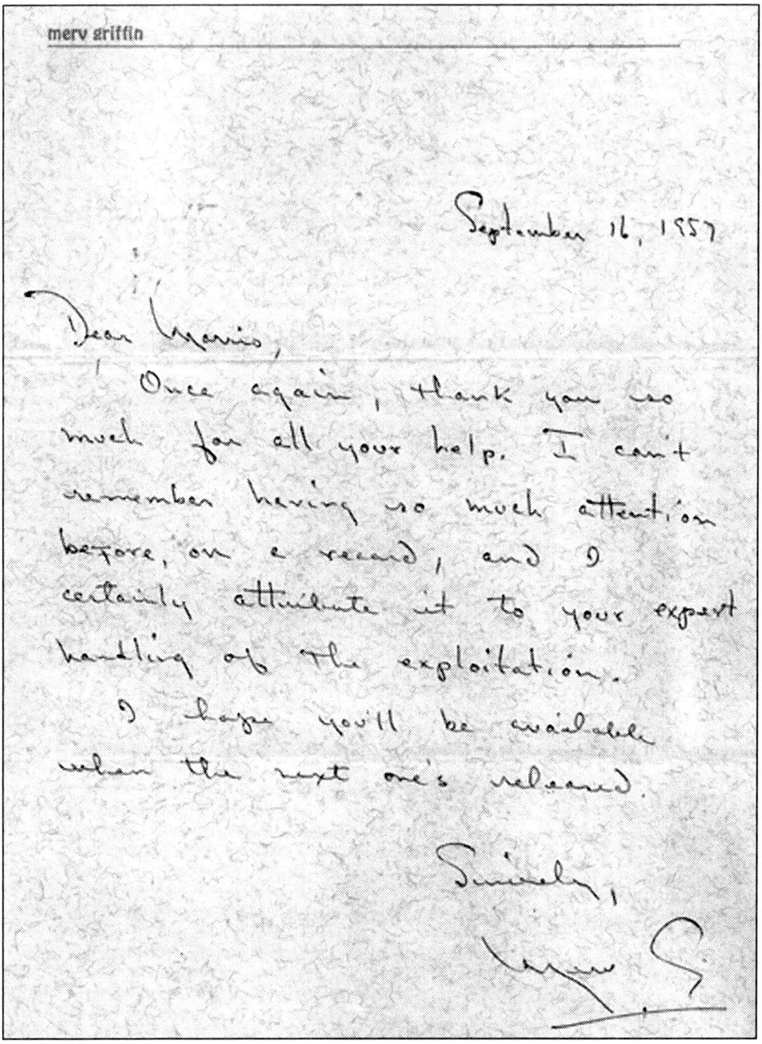

merv griffin

September 16, 1957

Dear Morris,

Once again, thank you so much for all your help. I can't remember having so much attention before on a record, and I certainly attribute it to your expert handling of the exploitation.

I hope you'll be available when the next one's released.

Sincerely,

Merv G.

A cherished and gentlemanly gesture from Merv Griffin. A thank you note. The only other thank you note I ever received was from Dinah Shore.

I attended a National Academy of TV Arts and Sciences luncheon in La Quinta, California in April, 2006, where Merv was inducted and presented with the Gold and Silver Award for 50 years of service in the entertainment industry. It was there that he presented me with a coconut (see photo) commemorating our coconut association of years ago regarding his recording of the same name. Which, of course, was Lovely and a whole bunch.

Merv Griffin presenting me with a Coconut to commemorate the 50th anniversary of his hit record, "I've Got A Lovely Bunch of Coconuts."

When many of us hung out at Caffe Roma in Beverly Hills, Merv would pop in for lunch every once in a while, come over to our table and make me look like a big shot. He always thanked me for the job I did on his hit record.

We did remain friends through the years. I felt privileged to be invited to his funeral on August 17, 2007 at the Church of Good Shepherd in Beverly Hills.

Chapter Twelve
PAUL KAPP

It boggles my mind. Just on a hunch, I googled The Kapp Brothers. There were pages of data on Jack and Dave Kapp. Jack, as we all know started Decca Records in 1934. In 1943, he startled the industry by recording the Broadway stage hit, *Oklahoma,* which paved the way for other record companies to follow suit and add Broadway show cast albums to their catalog. When he died at the age of 49, his brother Dave took over as the head of the label. David was very entrepreneurial, having been in management and other aspects of the entertainment industry. He later started his own label, Kapp Records. It further boggles my mind. The point I'm getting at is that when you Google 'The Kapp Brothers," you will find pages and pages of the two brothers, but not a single mention of brother Paul Kapp. There's even a mention of a Bertha Kapp, a sister who was peripherally involved with brother David. Paul struggled his way to whatever success he had, and he ultimately did have a good share of his 15 minutes in the sun, but with no help at all from his brothers.

Paul Kapp was a composer/music publisher, General Music, ASCAP. I contracted to work for him as a song-plugger for one year, 1950. He was a struggling publisher, as for example, his co-writer, Moe Jaffe worked in the office performing menial jobs along with Paul's wife. Strictly a family affair.

We had success with an Arthur Godfrey recording of Burl Ives, "Little White Duck." I played it for Archie Bleyer, conductor of the radio show and Will Roland, producer of the CBS show. Godfrey performed the song initially on his show and was pleased enough at the reaction to want to record it for Columbia Records. It did very well.

When the record was released, Paul Kapp had an idea and asked me if I would want to go to some "out of the city" radio stations and see if I can get them to play the Godfrey record. Initially, I went to Poughkeepsie, Newark, Albany, Hartford and New Haven. I loved it. Not only because I was able to get a lot of airplay, but in most cases they were so happy to see a "song-plugger," the disc jockeys and program directors bought me lunch.

It was then that I decided that when my one year agreement with Paul Kapp ended, I would go into independent record promotion. Which I did. But later for that.

Back to the saga of Paul Kapp. At the termination of my agreement with Paul, I left the company; his wife was stricken with cancer. She knew she had a short time to live and decided to go to Belgium and visit her daughter who was married to a young man that worked for the US Embassy in Belgium. While visiting, they were all invited to a party at the Embassy where she was approached by a gentleman who remarked "I understand your husband is a very famous music publisher in America." A little embarrassed, she told him that Paul was a music publisher, but wasn't too sure as to how famous he was. Nonetheless, he proceeded to give her a package of music to bring back to the States and give to Paul. She had no idea what kind of music was in the package, but agreed to take it to her husband.

The package contained the many songs performed by a Belgian Nun, aka Sister Luc aka Jeanine Deckers, and finally aka'd as The Singing Nun. Aside from the hit recording on Philips, the song, Dominique, was recorded by thirty-two artists from all over the world. One of the most prominent was by the international duo, Sandler and Young.

Mrs. Kapp returned home to the States and handed the package over to Paul. He was able to acquire worldwide publishing rights to the music. Unfortunately his wife didn't live long enough to taste the fruit of her efforts and enjoy the success of it all.

It was as though God sent her on her last mission to Belgium to get the music and help her husband's fledgling music company see some daylight financially.

A short while later, a mid-west corn-belt disc jockey pulled a cut from a new Tony Bennett album that was published by General

Music and played the heck out of it. The play mushroomed from state to state to country to country to become one of the biggest hits of all time. "I Left My Heart in San Francisco." Again, Paul's wife didn't live long enough to enjoy the success that the song garnered.

About four months after I left the job with General Music, I received a lovely surprise in the form of a check from Paul Kapp. I had forgotten that part of our agreement for the year was for me to participate in the ASCAP earnings. Paul didn't forget.

He passed away in 1976. I certainly will never forget him. A true mensch.

Chapter Thirteen
PIC RECORDS

Don't try to Google Pic Records. All you'll find is Epic Records, but my story is only about Pic Records.

During my Independent Promotion years of the mid-50s, I was hired by a gentleman who started the label and wanted to wade in the waters of the record business. His name, Joe Piccola.

I knew nothing about Joe—who he was, where he came from—what his past experiences about owning a record company...nothing. But what I was soon to find out, scared the shi-laly out of me. Joe was a good looking guy in his 50s, tall and very impressive looking. His background? Well, that's another story...or still the same story.

In his younger years, Joe Piccola was one of Mafia chief, Frank Costello's, lieutenants. Whether, at that time, he had any association with past associates, I couldn't tell you. He seemed to be doing everything according to Hoyle and wanted to do his best to make records and be a part of our world.

Our head of A & R at Pic Records was legendary arranger/conductor, Don Costa, who, as we all know, in his later years arranged and conducted for Frank Sinatra and also Steve Lawrence & Eydie Gorme. We had a modicum of success with airplay and sales. I set up distribution and the cooperation from the distributors nationwide was as good as any other labels the distributors represented. It had to be or if not I'd have their legs broken—just kidding.

At one time I did go on a promotion road trip and Joe insisted I take an "associate" with me who wanted to learn the business. His name was Frankie—and a recent parolee. We shared a room at the hotel in Pittsburgh. We were taken to our room and after the bellboy left, Frankie placed his suitcase on his bed and opened it. There in broad daylight was a .45 revolver lying neatly among his clothes. I asked him, "What is this all about?" His reply was simply, "You never know what can happen."

Well, thankfully, nothing every happened. He was a friendly sort and I didn't mind his company, but I think his presence during my pitching my records to program directors and disc jockeys on the road trip did enhance the airplay of product on Pic records considerably.

A few weeks later, back home safely in The Bronx, I got a call from Joe Piccola who asked if I was going to come into Manhattan that day. I told him I expected to and then invited me to lunch with him and a couple of his friends at Patsy's very famous Italian restaurant on West 56th street "and we'll be eating in the kitchen" I was informed.

Sitting and having lunch in Patsy's kitchen made me feel very privileged—as was Frank Sinatra and many celebrities when they wanted privacy during their meals with close friends. I felt very comfortable lunching with Joe and his four buddies. What their association with Joe was, I never asked, except that their conversations about their families and past adventures were very interesting and entertaining at the same time.

A gentleman was sitting opposite me and I was noticing his wrist watch mainly because of the gold cover. He caught me eyeing the watch, removed it and handed it over to me. I clicked open the gold lid and the face of the time piece added beauty to it. After eyeing it for a minute or two, I returned the watch to him. He wouldn't take it. "Keep it, kid" was his reply. I showed him the watch on my wrist and I thanked him anyway. He insisted that I keep it. I looked at Joe, and he gave me a look to say "Keep it." I kept it!

The owner of the watch, I ultimately found out, was James (Jimmy Jerome) Squillante, I learned later was "King of the garbage collection racket." I was also told that he was due to testify in Albany before a committee on Garbage Collection in Queens, New York the week after the lunch. Go know. He was very gentlemanly and if I didn't have an idea as to who he really was, I don't think that I would have had a thought about his actual background with the mob. I still have that watch and treasure it. It was only a short time after that Jimmy was "put out of his misery." His body was never found.

Pic Records lasted for about a year. I lost track of Joe Piccola after he disposed of the company and its masters, and I'd lie if I didn't say it was a great learning experience in discovering the good in personalities of people—all sorts of people.

Chapter Fourteen
TELLY SAVALAS

Whodathunkit? I'm going back to the fifties when Telly Savalas was directing and producing an all-night disc jockey show on ABC radio. You remember radio, don't you? The disc jockey who helmed the show was a one-armed talent by the name of Gene Stewart. Last I heard, Gene was into sports and doing the color for the New York Rangers ice hockey team. Enough of Gene. Back to Telly.

As an indy record promoter living in New York at the time, it was destined that part of my appointed rounds was to get the records of my clients played on Gene Stewart's midnight show on ABC radio. That being the case and acting according to PPP (proper promotional protocol), I dared not go directly to the disc jockey to beg for the plugs, but the correct thing to do was go to the person actually responsible for adding my clients' records...enter my hero, Telly Savalas, Gene's producer/director.

We carried on a normal every day producer/plugger relationship, such as, "Hey Telly, let's go bowling before you go to work," or "let's grab a bite." Those were but a few of the obvious tricks of the trade to have our wares aired. This relationship remained on a solid footing for all the years until his death at the age of 70 in January, 1994. I was at his bedside, my hand on his shoulder, along with his loving family as the priest was giving him the last rites.

While at Mercury Records in Chicago, our west coast A & R head, Quincy Jones scored a film titled *Love is a Ball*. We had scheduled the release of the soundtrack for the film which starred Telly. The producer of the film was Marty Poll who, up until five years prior, had been a song-plugger colleague. The publicist for the film was

1961, L-R ex music publisher-turned film producer, Marty Poll, Me, Telly and wife # 2, Lynn.

concocting a national press junket to Las Vegas. I, in turn, concocted a contest for the listeners to Marty Faye's disc jockey show in Chicago. That won me four seats on the chartered jet that was schlepping the local paparazzi from our Chicago to Las Vegas. It was there that I renewed my old friendship with Telly and where I met wife #2, Marylynne Savalas, nee Gardner. We spent the couple of days in Vegas together just reminiscing and, generally, having a ball.

A few months later, it was Academy Awards time. I had arrived in L.A. a day before. The publicist, who worked on the film that took me to Vegas, on parting, asked me to give him a call "whenever you're in town." I did. I called him on the Monday morning the day the Oscars were to be given out to just say "hi" and keep our association intact.

Timing is everything. Twenty minutes before I phoned him he got a call from one of his clients advising him that he will not be able to attend the awards that evening. He wasn't feeling well with a strep throat and to give his tickets to someone else. The prized hard-tickets belonged to Burt Lancaster. Seventh row center—and I was given the tickets. This is at ten o'clock in the morning.

I was supposed to spend the day with Mercury's west coast sales manager, and one of my closest friends, Tom Bonetti, visiting radio stations, record stores, etc. Instead, we frantically and panic stricken to a point, got fitted for a tuxedo, prettied up at the Beverly Hills Health Club where Tom was a member, rented a car (imagine us pulling up in front of the Santa Monica Civic Auditorium in a red Volkswagen sandwiched between the armada of chauffeur driven limos, and us two schnooks get out to walk the red carpet into the venue. Photographers weren't sure whether to snap our picture or not.

Telly was nominated for Supporting Role in the film *Birdman of Alcatraz*. He was beaten out of the award by Ed Begley Jr. Frank Sinatra was the MC at the event. After the show was over and we trekked over to the huge tent to attend the Governor's Ball mingling with the best that Hollywood had to offer. Tom and I were in awe and stretching our necks to see who else we can see when in comes a bunch of photographers with flashbulbs shooting off at machine-gun speed preceding Sinatra's entrance to the ball. Frank spotted me, walked away from his entourage, and said, "You—out." Pointing a thumb towards the door...then a hug and said..."Hi, Moishe," and went on his way to his table, and so did we to ours. My friend, Tom, was flabbergasted and talks about that experience in his life to everyone.

The next few years I visited California a number of times each year in the line of duty. Each time I came to L.A., there was always a point where Telly and I got together...never losing touch. Now his career was really booming. He was always working. A TV drama, a series, movies always working. Along with his booming career came an insatiable appetite for Las Vegas.

Telly was the fan's best friend. He would go out of his way to please his public. Often times when we'd be at lunch or dinner, inevitably s pretty young thing would come along and ask if she could take his picture. To her pleasant surprise, he would grab the fan, put her on his lap and hand the camera over to me to snap the photo of him and her. I recall also that while filming *Kojak* at Universal, he would take his lunch break by driving his golf cart on his way to his bungalow deliberately zeroing in on the area where tourists gathered to take their Universal Studios tour causing havoc while he paused for photos and autographs. The powers that be that ran the tour department rewarded Telly with a case of vodka for being the most cooperative personality with the tourists.

When he got word from CBS TV that the two hour movie of the week, *The Marcus Nelson Murders* would become a TV series featuring him with the title lead as Kojak, he phoned to tell me the good news and added two words, "Use me." Which actually meant for me to call on him for whatever favor I might need; he prophesized his future. He knew that the new series would be a hit…did it ever! He couldn't go anywhere in the world without being recognized and he loved every minute of it.

He used his influence with his producer to cast friends and relatives on the show from time to time. His brother, George, who played detective Stavros, became a personality as did his good friend, photographer, Vince Conti, who played Detective Rizzo. Another good friend was composer/arranger John Cacavas, who was hired as the composer/arranger for the TV show.

Telly was even instrumental in having me join the Screen Actors Guild so I could grab a part here and there on *Kojak*. At one time, I played the part of a doorman, another was in Chinatown and I was one of the detectives going in on a raid. Or I'd just be another cop at the typewriter in the police station. The one I enjoyed most was when they dubbed my voice in a police car advising the officers about a crime taking place. For a few years I was making as much as $3.29 yearly on residuals for the six shows I worked in. I knew for sure that this wasn't going to be my life's ambition. But I did have fun.

I spent many years as surrogate husband and father to his wives, Lynn and later on Julie as well as surrogate father to his children while he was away filming in some foreign country. They were all fun to be with and appreciative at the same time for the attention I would give them. As well, because of my association with Telly, I had become friendly with the mother of his son, Nicholas and her daughter Nicolette, who as a child used to call me Uncle Morey. With her British accent, it sounded adorable. Nicolette, later on, got into acting and initially used the name of Savalas, but changed it to Sheridan when she was advised that she couldn't use Savalas because her mother and Telly never wed and she was not Telly's daughter. As it is, she did hit it big landing a big part on the *Desperate Housewives* TV show as Nicolette Sheridan along with a number of other films TV shows.

Telly loved to gamble. When I first moved to L.A. in the mid-60s, I hung out with Telly quite a bit. At that particular time he was being wooed by the entertainment director at Caesar's Palace to star as Tevya in their upcoming production of *Fiddler On The Roof.* Actually, that was his excuse to drive to Vegas every other weekend for "talks" about the show, and, shouldn't be a total loss that he was already in Vegas; he would show his presence in the casino. It was almost mixed emotions for the brass at Caesar's Palace...are they entertaining him and his entourage for the Fiddler production, or are they just content to have him as "star attraction" in the casino...to all the other gamblers delight. Either way they were pleased to have him and his entourage and those in his entourage benefited by all the perks.

A great part of my years with Telly was when Paramount Pictures producer, Howard Koch, bought a horse and asked Telly if he wanted to go partners with him. Howard had initially asked his buddy, Walter Matthau, but he declined. This happened in the early '70s. The cost was $3,000 each. Telly bought in. They named the horse "Telly's Pop." The horse, against all odds, won race after race. Telly's Pop was forced into retirement with a chipped hoof just two months before a scheduled run in the Kentucky Derby on April 5, 1976. He did that well. Up to that point, the total earnings were $353,995. Not a bad profit. Telly had been asked to serve as Grand Marshall at Churchill Downs and he kept his promise even though his horse was eliminated. He took me and another friend, Hal Taines. We were treated like royalty with police escorts, mint-julep parties all over the place, breakfast and lunch with the Governor of Kentucky...the whole enchilada. We were also invited to a stable to watch how they assist horses in mating. Not that it was embarrassing, but I turned all colors when in walks a nun, herding a class of school children to watch horses...for want of a better word...mate. A most memorable weekend.

The trip of a lifetime came when I convinced an associate of mine from Holland to take Telly into a studio and record an album. My friend was an exceptionally good record promoter in Europe...his

Me, entrepreneur Hal Taines, and Telly hitting the chow line at one of the receptions at Churchill Downs in Louisville, KY in the 1976 running of the Kentucky Derby. Our host, Kentucky Governor Wendell Ford can be seen between Hal and Telly.

name was Charley Prick. I wanted to change his name to Harry Prick. At about the same time, Telly got an offer to come to Monte Carlo to televise a guest appearance on an American TV show filming there and produced by Marty Passetta. Scheduling-wise, that was fitting in nicely with our initial plans to go to Holland. The name of the TV show was, brilliantly titled, *The Monte Carlo Show*. In the midst of our planning, another notification arrives to Telly from an art dealer in the small hamlet named Beverly in Northern England. Telly's mother, Christina, was a wonderful artist and had some success with her paintings which led to an offer from the art dealer to hold an exhibit in one of the many art galleries in Beverly. Telly was asked if he could attend the opening of his mother's show of art. How could he refuse? This was to be part of the trip.

The first leg of the trip from L.A. to London, the cast of characters were: Telly, his wife Julie; her mother Gloria Hovland; my wife, Elena; and Telly's brother, Gus. When we arrived in London, we were met at Heathrow Airport by the art dealer in one car and an associate in another. Of course he was notified that there might be a cast of thousands and should be prepared to provide transportation accordingly. They wanted to immediately drive up to the town of Beverly. We thought better of this and Telly advised them that we should first go to his palatial London flat on Lowndes square, (which was my home away from home for many years), change clothes, unpack and repack just enough clothes for the two days in Beverly. That we did and went merrily on our drive up to Beverly.

In England, on most of the overpasses on their freeways, there are coffee shops and restaurants. Halfway on our trip, Telly decided he wanted to have some coffee and a rest stop. That was an experience. The restaurant was crowded and when Telly walked in, you'd think that Prince Charles appeared. It was hectic and the bald one loved every minute of it. We continued on our way to our destination directly to our hotel which was, as best as I can recall, the Beverly Arms. Just on the outskirts of the city. Management did manage to tell us that Her Majesty, the Queen, always sent Princess Margaret to this hotel every year for a holiday. We loved it.

The next morning we attended a reception in their city hall hosted by the mayor and her consort husband. It was lovely and charming. That was followed by a parade through the city given by the local police department and gave the natives a chance to wave at Telly and Julie as they waved back. We wisely opted to watch the parade as any another Beverly-ite. We waited and trekked over to the Art Gallery for the official opening of Christina Savalas' Art Show. It was a very successful opening and everyone was pleased.

We all begged off the drive back to London and opted for the rails. It was a fun and comfortable train ride back to the flat.

With three bedrooms and three baths and a few sleepable sofas, we all managed to get some rest before we took a flight the next morning to Nice for Marty Pasetta's Monte Carlo TV show.

Joining us in Monte Carlo was "Kojak's" conductor, arranger, composer, John Cacavas and his wife Bonnie. John rehearsed Telly on the tune he would perform on the TV show and also conducted the orchestra as well. The tune was "Nevertheless." When we landed at the Nice Airport, we were met by two limos who would take us to Monte Carlo and Hotel De Paris. Bonnie and John arrived ahead of us. The chauffeurs greeted us, gathered our luggage and directed us to the limos. At that time they also handed each of us a credit card. This card was sponsored by the TV show and the Societe des Baines de Mer, Monaco. It allowed each of us entertainment courtesies to the tune of $600 daily…not including the hotel suites and rooms that we occupied at the Hotel De Paris which was another great perk. The card gave us access to the Monte Carlo Sporting Club, restaurants and other advantages that were too numerous to take advantage of in the short time we were in Monte Carlo. I thought I died and landed in Heaven. Southern France has since become my favorite vacation spot in the world. Although Paris is a beautiful city, the Parisians can't hold a candle to the citizens of Southern France and the Riviera. A big difference in personalities and attitude.

The Monte Carlo show filmed a different guest almost daily. While we were there, we shared stories with Charles Aznavour, Doc Severinson, Hal Linden, Dionne Warwick, among others who were all sharing their good fortune of being a guest in this wonderful little country.

After spending a fulfilled, fun-filled week in Monaco, it was now time for our little caravan to schlep up to Amsterdam and to our recording studio in Hilversum to record an album for Charley Prick and Papagaya Records. We landed in Amsterdam and again, two limos brought us to the Amstel Hotel on the Amstel River, where, while checking in, the manager took pride in showing us and Telly his check-in log of many years ago…with signatures by Franklin D. Roosevelt, Winston Churchill and everyone's favorite, Adolph Hitler.

While John, Telly and I slaved away in the recording studio for many hours every day, Charley Prick arranged for the limo driver to take our ladies on tour. They went to the diamond factory, museums, windmills and lunches. Didn't cost them or us a nickel. Good old Charley came through no matter what people say about his last name. After each session we all gathered at a predetermined restaurant and have our dinner together. One dinner that was outstanding was in a windmill.

I remember it was about 9:30 in the evening and the sun was still out there. After dinner we would all gather in Telly's suite for a goodnight shot of Jong Jenever (young gin) my favorite drink in Holland. Telly had a little quirk that used to irritate my wife…and

In Vegas—Telly and Julie Savalas, Elena and Morris Diamond and everyone's favorite European record promoter, Charley Prick.

me. He would start a discussion about anything...politics, sports. After about twenty minutes, there we are, John, Gus, Telly and I arguing and screaming at each other...it's not a discussion any longer, it's an argument. As soon as Telly saw that the argument he started had gotten to a feverish pitch...he retreated into his bedroom and went to sleep, leaving us in a state of frenzy. The next day when we confronted him, in his best academy award acceptance tone he declared "Me? I don't remember starting anything." This generally went on four nights a week.

We finished the album, went back to London for a couple of days, and then back to California. When the album was finally released, I was sent a few copies and noticed in the credits that I was listed in the "many thanks to" category along with the limo drivers, the guy that ran out for coffee, and some other unidentifiable characters. I went ballistic. I was supposed to be listed as exec producer and Charley (the) Prick as producer. I had my lawyer contact the record company but it was too late for the initial release to be called back, but the problem was resolved on future releases. The album sold over 4,000,000 in Europe.

Yes, that was the trip of a lifetime. Beverly, England; Monte Carlo, Monaco; Amsterdam, Holland. One that I cherish dearly and daily.

Now back home and Telly's back at work shooting *Kojak* for another season. He got his two Golden Globe awards and was beginning to settle down a little. He was invited to many celebrity golf tournaments. He was a good golfer. There was a time when an organization in Phoenix decided to hold a Telly Savalas Golf Tournament for a local Greek charity.

Many of his buddy-actors attended to play golf to be part of a four-some with local prominent business people who shelled out $2,500 per person for the privilege...the bucks of course, went to the charity. I've always played tennis and never really had the knack of golfing. However, he insisted I play as a celebrity in one of the foursomes. Here three prominent schnooks from local Phoenix businesses were putting up $2,500 each for the privilege of playing with me, Moishe.

I told them I was not really a golfer, which they found out for themselves early enough; however, I was good at putting. At the eleventh hole, it was my turn to try and sink a twenty footer from the fringe of the green. I sunk it. They picked me up and put me on their shoulders and said that I saved the day for them. Next time I putt on the green, I think I'll keep my eyes closed again. Telly was proud of me.

I was part of a poker game that included a music lawyer (Neil Fischer), a manufacturer of record albums (Bill Pine), an ophthalmologist (Shelly Coburn), a gynecologist (Steve Pine, Billy's brother), a record company exec (Alan Mink), a garment center rep (Bill Bosch), an actor (Telly Savalas). A mixture of characters that could never be duplicated by the most famous of casting directors. We had a ball. Telly would cancel engagements so that, G-d forbid, he shouldn't miss a game, and we all felt the same way. This was a must attend every week not because we had to—we wanted to. The comradeship couldn't be duplicated. One evening we had a big laugh when the gynecologist said to the eye doctor "How disgusting and boring it must be for you to do nothing but look into people's eyes all day every day." Huge laugh!

For a number of years I ran the Music Industry Tennis Tournaments. This was a gathering of everyone involved in music: music publishers,

Telly Savalas helping me co-host the Music Industry Tennis Tournaments.

record company execs, disc jockeys, lawyers, accountants, various suppliers, recording artists, composers. When I mentioned the new venture to Telly, he asked if he could be my co-host. I said it would be ok, but that he would physically have to attend the tournaments which were generally a three day weekend at some tennis ranch or tennis club or anyplace that would have more than fifteen tennis courts that could accommodate our needs. That was ok with him. He was also a good tennis player, but he enjoyed watching the matches as well as participating in our closing cocktail party and dinner by helping in presenting the awards. We did that for about twelve years.

Telly called and wanted to know if I wanted to meet him at the TV studio on Vine Street where Merv Griffin was taping his show. I joined him in the green room where he had himself his usual healthy full glass of vodka before appearing before an audience. I joined him with a glass of merlot. After the show, we went to a nearby Italian restaurant on Melrose and Highland and were joined by his girlfriend, Sally Adams. We had a lovely dinner and more wine. Telly was living in Beverly Hills and I was living in Encino at that time. We both consumed a good amount of liquor. On my way home, I was stopped on the Ventura Freeway by the Highway Patrol. They said I was weaving a bit. I had to get out of my car and walk a straight line. Jokingly I told one of the officers that I won't walk the line unless they put a net under it. He sort of laughed and asked me to blow into the palm of his hand…I did and told him that I hoped I didn't melt his ring…again, sort of a snicker. He felt that he had to take me in for further testing. They cuffed me. One officer drove my car off the freeway and parked it on Van Nuys Boulevard and we all went to the police station further up to the Van Nuys City Hall. At this point I was fairly sober and was asking very legitimate questions such as what percentage in the breathometer do I have to reach to be cleared or arrested and our conversations were clear and intellectual. When we got inside the police station there were all kinds of drunks hollering and making a mess of things. They gave me the breathometer test and said I was a bit over the .09 limit. The two cops huddled and decided to let me go free because I didn't hassle them and felt that I could get home safely. They drove me to my car and I drove home with no problem.

The next day I went and had lunch with Telly on his lunch break from shooting at Universal. I told him of my experience of the night before. He laughed. The same thing happened to him while driving to his home in Beverly Hills.

He was stopped on Melrose by a motor cycle cop for weaving. The cop asked Telly's girlfriend if she could drive and she told him she could. He then told Telly that he couldn't give a "fellow cop" a ticket and suggested he let his friend drive.

An almost similar situation occurred while we were driving to Vegas. In the car was Telly—who has to drive no matter whose car we're in, me and *The Untouchables* co-star, Paul Picerni. Telly was speeding and we got stopped by this storm trooper somewhere near Barstow. Telly was wearing black slacks and a black silk shirt that was buttoned at the collar. He was issued a citation from the cop with an admonition to "drive carefully, Father." Here was the only person in the world that not only didn't recognize Telly; he didn't acknowledge his name when he wrote out the citation. That pissed off Telly more than getting the ticket.

Telly felt good about his life. He enjoyed it, obviously. He was always good to his fans and regarded all of them as an integral part of his success. He respected them and never tried to avoid or shun them at any time. As a matter of fact, he would go out of his way to accommodate them.

In his last couple of months, I spent much time with him in his apartment at the Sheraton Universal in Universal City. A week before he died, I was sitting on the edge of his bed and his nurse was helping him put on the long stockings. He turned, kissed me on the back of my head and said "My dear friend, Moishe." A week later on a Saturday morning, I had just finished playing tennis and drove over to the Sheraton Universal to visit Telly. I knocked on the door of the suite and his oldest daughter, Christina, opened the door and told me to go into the bedroom as the priest was giving Telly his last rites. Standing around the bed as Telly was taking his last breath, were his children, Christina, Candace, Penelope, Ariana, Christian and Nicholas; his brother Gus; his wife Julie and myself. This was January 24, 1994...a day after his 70th birthday.

Do I miss him? What do you think?

Chapter Fifteen
MORTON DOWNEY, JR.

Morton Downey, Jr. and I go back to our early years when he was writing songs and trying to get to the popularity status his father, Morton Downey, Sr., attained in the '30s and '40s as an Irish Tenor on stage, recordings and radio. I was a measly song plugger and Mort was just another hopeful songwriter hanging out in front of the Brill Building, the mecca of music publishers on Broadway.

I did manage to self-publish a few songs he had written. I also got him a one-shot record deal with Kapp Records.

We really locked in with each other in the early '60s after I moved to Chicago and Mercury Records and he was getting a bit of a reputation as a disc jockey. He was living in Chicago as well.

As a disc jockey, he made a lot of waves...some good and some not so good. He never held a job more than six months or a year. There would always be some controversy that would cause him to call me to ask if there were any program directors that are looking for a DJ. Part of my job was to ride herd on the record promoters that worked for Mercury's thirty-three record distributors—the other part was to get on the phone myself and contact DJs and program directors to stay in touch and also to get the latest scoop from their end.

Mort had jobs in radio in Buffalo, Connecticut, and Miami that I had organized. His last job was in Miami and here is why it was his last job. The Beatles were in town. Mort went on the air to make that announcement, but he also mentioned on the air that Paul McCartney was staying at the home of the competing program director and proceeded to give the PD's home phone number on the air. You can imagine the havoc that caused.

Morton Downey, Jr. being interviewed by Gene Kaye of Allentown, Pa., who did his weekend shows at Grossingers in the Catskills. I booked the recording artists for Gene's weekend shows and that gave me a free-bee at the famous Grossingers every weekend. Wow!

When he was in Buffalo, he placed a full page ad in the number one industry trade magazine, *Billboard*, announcing his good ratings at the radio station he had attained. I saw the ad and thought that was a good idea. UNTIL—a few days later Mercury Records received a bill in the mail from *Billboard* for three thousand dollars, the price for the ad. Needless to say I was put on the carpet by my bosses.

I then called *Billboard* and told them that we are not paying for the ad inasmuch as we didn't authorize or order it. They said that Downey ordered it and told them to bill Mercury. Of course that was a stupid comeback and they knew better of it and backed off and took the loss.

Mort came back to Chicago and fell in love with a Playboy Bunny/Model. He was truly infatuated with Lori and they set a wedding date. I was asked to be his best man. The day before the wedding, there was the traditional rehearsal in the Catholic Church plus dinner.

The priest approached Mort and mentioned that he didn't think it would be appropriate for me to be best man because I was Jewish and not proper for me to enter the altar area. Mort asked the priest "How much did my father donate to the church for the wedding?" The priest replied, "Ten thousand dollars." Mort told him he felt that amount should cover my coming up to the altar during the ceremony.

The priest was beside himself. He then asked me if I would kneel as I entered the altar. I told him I didn't think that would be proper. He then asked if I'd bow. Same answer. In a state of frustration, he asked if I'd nod as I entered the altar and I said "Ok, Father." It's a good thing I was at Mort's side during the ceremony. I had to nudge him when to kneel and when to stand up. All went well and it was a beautiful ceremony and affair and Lori was mind-bogglingly beautiful.

Mort was very locked in with the Kennedy clan. He spent much time in Washington, D.C. I know for a fact that if I ever wanted to get in touch with him, I would call Senator Ted Kennedy's office in Washington, ask for Mort, and sure enough, there he would be.

More years passed and now out of a clear blue sky, here's Mort known as a combative-talk-show host on national TV emanating from WOR-TV in Manhattan. It was a hit show that many believe paved the way for such type shows as *Jerry Springer*. Many of his guests were weirdoes. He would go face to face with them going so far as to blowing smoke in their face while chatting. It was a different type of TV and quite successful.

I decided to phone him. After a few tries, I finally reached his office that was at the WOR-TV transmitter in New Jersey. I tried to explain to his secretary who I was and to just tell him my name...which she did. Dead silence on the phone, and then his first words—"I knew you'd come crawling." That was typical of his sense of humor. This was in the late '80s.

Mort returned to Los Angeles and we renewed our friendship with lunches and dinners and had much fun talking about our professional adventures through the years.

Mort was an excessive smoker. He lost a lung to lung cancer in 1967 and paid the price for smoking heavily throughout his life when he died in March 2001 at the fairly young age of 67. He was a different kind of friend…but always a friend…good or bad. It saddened me to see him in such a condition when I would visit him at Cedars Sinai Hospital in Los Angeles.

I spoke at his funeral in North Hollywood and related the story of when I was best man at his wedding and what went on in the Church with the priest at the wedding rehearsal. It brought an air of much needed humor to a somber afternoon.

Chapter Sixteen
DAVID COMMONS

Mort Fleischmann was VP of RCA Corporate Public Relations that involved in making nice to the press on behalf of RCA Records, NBC TV, any satellite or other toys that had RCA components.

While browsing through his daily trade magazines, he noticed that a gent by the name of David Commons was preparing to direct a new film, *The Angry Breed* and was in the process of casting the film. This happened in 1968.

Mort, not wanting to get involved in pitching an act, asked if I'd try to contact David on his behalf and present him with the press kit telling one and all about his girl friend, Tondea Willis. She and her sister, Andra Willis, was featured on the Lawrence Welk TV show, and Andra was equally talented and attractive. She was married to Roy Kohn.

I located and had a meeting with David. He thought she was cute, but not right for any of the parts that remained open at that time. We then discussed the possibility of me being his music supervisor on the film. David said, "On one condition—I'll give you the job, but I want you to play the part of a producer in the film."

I said that I would like that, but I'm not an actor. "Don't worry about that, I'll walk you through the part and you'll be good," he said. Again, I repeated that I'm not an actor. He threatened me with "If you want the job it's yours only if you play the part I'd like you for in the film and that's it." I told him to call my agent, which he thought was very funny. So did I. I played the part and I was not bad. Legendary Mike Curb was my partner in putting together the music for the film.

Here I am an actor (?) in David's film *The Angry Breed*. Sharing the screen with me are Jan Sterling and Jan Murray. 1968."

David was a short man with a lovely white chin beard and moustache, and a super sense of humor. The film had a great cast—William Windom, James MacArthur, Jan Sterling, Jan Murray and yours truly. Yep, I even get cast credit besides a nice line in the credits as music supervisor.

I had brought my mother-in-law, Polly Sims, along to one of the shoots and he fell in like with her. Every time there was a shoot there was also a request to "bring the family." It wasn't a serious affair according to his wife.

This film was the only one he directed, having been a special effects man for seventeen features in the '50s and '60s.

The Angry Breed, I'm happy to say, did very well. After a decent theatrical release, it did enjoy a good run for a number of months on Showtime TV.

It didn't do much to bolster my career as an actor—didn't hurt either. But what was really nice was the income from the music of the film which was appreciated by both mine and Mike Curb's Music Publishing Companies.

Chapter Seventeen
CHITTY CHITTY BANG BANG

Mike Connors was head of promotion for Decca Records. We began our friendship in the mid '50s when he hired me to promote Peggy Lee's records after she left Capitol Records and joined Decca.

Mike left Decca a few years later when actor Jeff Chandler asked him to come to California and be his manager. I had just moved to L.A. myself a couple of years prior and we carried on our friendship.

After a short time, he picked up the songwriting team of Richard and Bob Sherman. Signed them with Disney and they hit their first home run with *Mary Poppins*. It wasn't too long after when Mike called and told me that the boys are finishing work on a new film for Cubby Broccoli. I was happy for him because I thought they were going to compose the music for a James Bond film.

Mike explained to me that this new film will be the first and only non-James Bond film that Cubby would produce and wanted me involved. Even though the music is published by United Artist Music Publishing Company, Mike and Cubby felt that they needed someone that would be the liaison between the Sherman Brothers, the Music Publishing Company, The Record Company and the film company, UA.

I signed a one year agreement with Film producer, Cubby Broccoli and the head of United Artists pictures, David Picker, to work on *Chitty Chitty Bang Bang* as the international coordinator of music. Today that job would have been labeled as a music supervisor. The only difference being that I not only worked the music with the Sherman Brothers, but also traveled worldwide to get the various songs recorded.

L-R: Albert R. "Cubby" and Dana Broccoli, Me, Tony Bennett, who recorded one of the tunes from *Chitty Chitty Bang Bang*. We attended Tony's opening at the Coconut Grove in L.A. in 1966.

To be honest, when I was offered the job I wasn't sure that it was what I wanted, or better yet, was it something that I would succeed in doing. I got a demo of the score of the film. The first thing I did was call Sid Garris, who at one time was a DJ in Windsor, Ontario, known as "Symphony Sid," and now was in artists' management. I explained to him the project I've just taken on, telling about the music and cast starring Dick Van Dyke. He asked me to rush the demo to his office, as he was leaving for New Orleans in a few hours to be with one of his acts, The New Christy Minstrels. He phoned me the next day to tell me that everyone loved the music and that "The Minstrels want to do the first album of music from Chitty Chitty." That was the first one and it gave me the confidence to pursue other avenues.

My first trip to Europe, I met with Horst Jankowski in Stuttgart, Germany, whose recording of "A Walk in the Black Forest," was one of my pet projects at Mercury Records. He featured "Chitty Chitty Bang Bang" in his next album, as did Paul Mauriate in France. His previous big hit on Mercury was "Love is Blue." Many of the recordings were drop-ins from different A & R meetings in different countries. Tony Bennett recorded "Hush-a-bye Mountain" from the score. I went to Milan to meet with the Columbia Records branch and tried to talk them into releasing Tony's record from this "very important film." I succeeded and found out that this was the first record of Tony's that would be released in that territory.

I'm proud to say that I was personally able to achieve 104 different recordings worldwide on the music from *Chitty Chitty Bang Bang*, which has endeared me to the Shermnn Brothers. The job was sensational in that it offered me my first trip to Europe. I took advantage of the international contacts I made while serving as National Promotion Director of Mercury Records in the early '60s and for the most part, they all came through for me in helping to get recordings of the score of *Chitty*.

My first trip was for two weeks. When I returned, the powers that be asked me to make another elongated trip for six weeks, take my wife along, all expenses paid. As a matter of fact, we were royally received by the United Artists Pictures' reps all over Europe. Didn't have to reach for a quarter.

In traveling throughout the UK and Europe, I was always accompanied by either a rep from local UA MUSIC or local UA Films.

When it came time for The Oscars Academy Award show, we were pleased that the song itself was one of the nominees, but not the winner.

A few years after that experience, I was again involved with Mike Connors and the Sherman Brothers with their score from Jack Wrather's film of The Magic of Lassie. We did ok on that film, and again came in second as an Oscar nominee.

Attending screening of *Magic of Lassie*; Richard Sherman (he and Bob did the music for *Mary Poppins*), Producer, Jack Wrather, his wife, actress, Bonita Granville, and me. I was Music Supervisor of the film.

After listening to the record, Dick remarked that she's very pretty and she did a good job with "Till There Was You," but he felt that it really wasn't right for the show. I told him that I wouldn't argue with his decision; however, he'd be doing his network a huge favor by having Anita on his show as a guest and she can perform the tune then. After all, she was a fellow-ABC-TV performer on The Breakfast Club show. He thought for a few seconds and agreed with me and gave me a date for her appearance on *American Bandstand*.

A month later, I brought Anita to Philadelphia for her guest appearance on Bandstand. As she was performing, I kept my eye on Dick, hunched over his podium with his clasped hands below his chin as he searched for a visual reaction from his teen-age dancers and he found it.

After the show, Dick approached me and said "I will start playing this record tomorrow—you're on."

My hunch paid off. Dick played the record on every show for the next three months and broke it wide open. It hit all the pop charts and went gold. He also asked me to bring her to perform on his first Rock 'n Roll show in Los Angeles at the Hollywood Bowl in 1959.

At a subsequent disc jockey convention in Miami, sponsored by the Storz Radio Stations in 1959, Joe Carlton asked me to attend and make a big splash. Which I did. With a meager budget, I rented the poolside bar at the Americana Hotel that housed the convention and us conventioneers. I had a huge banner made which spread over the bar in full view of those who were attending and were taking in the pool area that told everyone to have a free drink and "Keep cool with Carlton."

I brought Anita to the convention. It was there that she met local DJ Bob Greene. They fell in love, got married and had children. My fault!

A few months later, I took Anita to Los Angeles for Dick's first Rock 'n Roll show at the Hollywood Bowl. Dick also asked me to bring Jack Scott to perform at the Bowl. This was on a weekend. I decided to take an extra day in L.A., and instead of returning to New York on Sunday night, I opted to go back on Tuesday. So on Monday morning, I went to our L.A. office and had breakfast with our Western regional director, Don Genson. He thought it would be a good idea to call our boss in New York and tell him that I'll stay for another day. Which I did.

Joe's response to me was that if I wouldn't be back by the next morning, and then I shouldn't come back at all. I asked him to recall his promise to me of getting a day off for every day that Dick Clark played Anita's record…his answer was still the same. I returned to New York that night.

Later that year, I had my first bleeding ulcer attack. Joe Carlton had a plaque on his desk that read, "I don't get ulcers, I give them." Truer words were never written. However, a year later when I had another bleeding ulcer attack, went back to the same VA hospital in The Bronx which is where I went the year before. The doctor's decision was to operate. Joe called my wife and said that he wants to get me out of the VA hospital and put me in the fashionable Mt. Sinai Hospital in Manhattan and he would have the number one stomach-ulcer doctor do the surgery and he would absorb all costs. My wife told Joe that it was very nice of him, but she knows that I wouldn't leave the VA hospital because I had complete faith in the doctors that were taking care of me.

As it so happens, at that time the VA hospital would engage an outside specialist to be in attendance at every major surgery that was being performed. By sheer coincidence, the outside doctor in attendance was the very same doctor that Joe Carlton was going to perform my surgery at Mt. Sinai Hospital.

Joe was Mr. Nice Guy…but didn't want to show it too often. It would spoil his image.

Chapter Nineteen
KENNY ROGERS

I terminated my career as an independent record promoter to go straight and take a legitimate job as National Promotion Director of a new record label, Carlton Records. We had success with a number of artists, not the least of whom was Anita Bryant. Joe Carlton had huge successes as head of A & R for Mercury and RCA records before starting his own label in 1958.

Our Southwest regional rep was a gent out of Houston, Texas, Leland Rogers. For a short time he would pitch us on a new recording artist on a small record label that was getting sales and airplay in and around Houston. Not bad recognition. The name of the artist was Kenneth Ray Rogers...yep, his kid brother. My boss, Joe Carlton, thought it wouldn't be a bad idea to take a shot with him and release a newly recorded song called "That Crazy Feeling."

I strayed away from the obvious and initially sent the new release to pop stations, instead of country. To everyone's pleasant surprise, the record took off and we started to get listings in the top 100 and many radio station charts. I then was able to go to Philadelphia and pitch the record to Dick Clark armed with the trade paper charts and the radio station charts from all over the country. Dick was convinced and gave me a date for Kenny to appear on the show a few weeks hence.

Not working on an extravagant budget, I set up radio and trade interviews for Kenny covering the New York area, and also worked our way to Philadelphia hitting stations in Newark and Trenton. Also to keep the expenses down, I had Kenny stay at my apartment in The Bronx...to my both daughters' delight, not to mention my boss, fending off hotel expenses. My older daughter, JoAnne,

Kenny Rogers chatting with Melissa Manchester and friend.

vividly recalls his bunking in our apartment in The Bronx as well as the subway and ferry tour around the tip of downtown Manhattan that we took with Kenny accompanied by my daughters, JoAnne and Allyn.

We arrived in Philly and Kenny did a wonderful job on *American Bandstand*. Dick was very pleased at the reaction and gave us a couple of months of constant airplay…which also gave us nice sales and additional chart activity.

Shortly after, Kenny had a limited stint with a label owned by him and his brother; then a go with the jazz group, The Bobby Doyle Trio; followed by The New Christy Minstrels...from there on to bigger and better things in films, recordings and personal appearances being in the capable hands of manager Ken Kragen. His gigantic step to fame.

Through the years, I would bump into Kenny at industry conventions and affairs. He was always extremely cordial and often he would put his arm around me and announce to anyone within earshot as to how I was responsible for the promotion of his first hit record that brought the name Kenny Rogers to the attention of the entertainment industry as well as the public. That always made me feel good...but then I would reply, "So how come you never mention that in the book you wrote?" His reply, "Out of sight, out of mind, but I love you."

Whenever we do see each other, there's always the conventional hug and kiss.

Chapter Twenty
BILL DANA

In 1960, I enjoyed the many perks I received while acting as sales and promotion manager of Hanover-Signature Records, co-owned by jazz legend producer, Bob Thiele and Steve Allen. By just associating with them was "perky" enough for me to enjoy the job.

The "Man on the Street" segment of Steve's TV show was, at that time, one of the main topics discussed at everyone's water cooler the morning after.

As a result, it was decided by Bob and Steve that we record and release an album by the different characters that became America's viewing habit.

The two albums that popped up high in sales and on the trade charts were Bill Dana's "Jose Jimenez" and Don Adam's "Mr. Football" (Leon Football). My favorite line in Don's album: "I believe that a coach and his quarterback go hand in hand...but not on the campus."

Bill Dana's album had nothing but favorite lines and expressions that were quoted daily. Especially when he would pronounce his "H" as "J" and, reversely, pronounce his "J" as "H"...as in "I studied Hewish in Jebrew school."

When we released Jose Jimenez, I took it upon myself, with Bob Thiele's blessing, to take this album on the road. To start with, I phoned a good buddy of mine, Dan Sorkin at WCFL radio in Chicago. He had the morning locked up in that city. I told him that I was coming in with a special new album and we made a date for lunch. He didn't even ask me who the artist was...just said c'mon in and we'll do lunch. Which we did.

He was truly intrigued at the thought of Bill Dana doing his Jose Jimenez character in an album after enjoying him so much on the Steve Allen TV show and was most anxious to give it a listen. Which he did...and loved it. He asked where I would go from Chicago and who would I see. I told him I was heading to San Francisco and see a few of the guys. He told me that I must see Don Sherwood at KSFO radio. He then picked up the phone and called Don at home to tell him that I'll be coming in with a new Jose Jimenez album and suggested that he should be delighted to be the first to have this album on air on the West Coast.

I flew into Frisco and met with Don, who is affectionately known on the air in the Bay Area as "Donny-Babe." He loved the album and told me it wasn't necessary for me to see the other DJs in San Francisco, because he would be the only one that would consistently play cuts from the LP every morning. As a courtesy, I did drop a copy of the album off to a few DJs in Frisco who I knew. Don also called Dick Whittinghill, a Los Angeles morning DJ at KMPC radio to expect a visit with me and will be pleased with the LP that I'll play for him. He also talked to Tess Russell, who was Whittinghill's assistant and programmer.

I met with both Tess and Dick the next morning after he got off the air and the reception couldn't have been better. They loved Bill Dana's LP and promised much airplay. And so did the other jocks at the station which included Gary Owens, Wink Martindale, Johnny Magnus and a few others.

I felt my non-stop flight back to New York City had me arrive an hour before the plane...that is how elated I was. The efforts of the trip showed up a few weeks later when our record distributors were ordering the album in large quantities. That, understandably, put a big smile on the faces of Bob Thiele and Steve Allen, not to mention Bill Dana. All very appreciative.

What followed was, and still is, a wonderful relationship with Bill, who as of this writing is hibernating in Nashville with his wife, Ev. Still very active with his one-man shows.

A bit of a P.S. to this story—I left Hanover-Signature Records in 1962 to take the job as National Promotion Director of Mercury/Philips Records in Chicago. In 1965 I got a call from Bill Dana..."Moishe, you must watch *Get Smart* this week when it airs."

Bill Dana always the center of attention—and this photo. I'm on the left along with producer, Larry Dorn.

No explanation, no reason for me not to watch that particular show...which wasn't necessary, because that was one of my favorite shows anyway.

The show aired and I watched it...the entire *Get Smart* episode was about a missing diamond..."Who stole the MORRIS Diamond?" was bantered throughout the show. I got many calls the next few days from friends and relatives figuring that the show was a dedication to me. I guess it was, in a sense, from Bill, who has always been associated with Don Adams and the show in one way or another. That made me proud.

It isn't too often that a record promoter falls in like with his client, but you can't help it with Bill Dana. I enjoyed working on his album mainly because of his sincere appreciation of the effort. Not too many recording artists are that way. Bill Dana one of a kind.

Chapter Twenty-One
STEVE ALLEN

In 1960, after serving for two years as National Promo Director of Carlton Records, I got a call from Bob Thiele, probably one of the most revered top Jazz A & R men in the business...he headed a record company which he partnered with Steve Allen; Hanover-Signature Records.

He was looking for a National Promotion Director and would I be interested enough to have lunch with him and talk about it. Which I did. I always had a huge admiration for Bob and his recordings through the years, not to mention my being a super fan of Steve Allen. I was flattered that he sought me out.

Steve was very hot at the time and busy helming the *Tonight Show* on NBC nightly. We came to the conclusion that we can't record Steve Lawrence and Eydie Gorme—or Andy Williams; who were all featured on the *Tonight Show* because by that time, other record companies had signed them.

After having some success with a couple of jazz artists ala Ray Brown, we decided to utilize the talents we had on the *Tonight Show* and record Don Adams, Bill Dana, Don Knotts Louis Nye, Tom Poston, Pat Harrington and a few others...notably, "The Man on the Street" gang, a popular feature of Steve's TV show.

These albums were most welcomed by disc Jockeys from all over the U. S. In particular was Bill Dana's *My Name, Jose Jimenez.* That was a major selling album more so because of radio air play along with the TV exposure from the *Tonight Show.*

I calculated at the time that many of the pop DJs around the country were in dire need of comedy relief on their shows, so I

Legendary Jazz producer and Steve's partner in Hanover-Signature Records, Bob Thiele, showing his distaste for the finer arts of my piano playing. Not so displeased is John VanDerBerg, General Manager of the label.

physically took the album right to their front door.

We followed that LP with a Don Adams album and a Man on the Street album all with great airplay and ultimately, great sales. Shortly after that, our sales manager, Irv Stimmler, left Hanover-Signature to join a new 20th Century-Fox label, which opened the door for Bob to promote me as sales manager along with my duties as National Promotion Director.

A few years later, in May, 1966, I made a move when I left Mercury that had been on my mind for a few years…to move to Los Angeles. Through a quirk of fate, I started getting involved in consulting music for films and TV.

After awhile, I set up an office in a small cottage adjoining the "Brill building of the West Coast" the 9000 building on Sunset Boulevard. By sheer coincidence, the only other tenant in the cottage was a film producer who was preparing a new movie. After exchanging a bunch of "hellos," he visited me in my office to find out what business I'm in. I basically told him, "Music."

Poof....I became his music supervisor on his upcoming film, *A Man Called Dagger*. By this time, Steve Allen was now back on the West Coast as well, and we had a few opportunities to see each other and chat. I told the producer that I knew Steve Allen, and would he want to consider Steve to do the music for his film. He was excited at the thought and added that he was sure that Steve would be too expensive. I told him I would check it out.

I was only a little reticent about talking to Steve, although he had successfully written a number of good songs for films, he never really got involved in actually scoring a full motion picture...underscore, back-ground, chases, etc. In my talking to Steve, he was confident he could come up with a good jazz score for the film.

I then suggested that his price might be too high...with name film composers charging at that time well over $50,000 just for scoring a film, aside from the musicians, arrangers and copyists. His reply to me was in the form of a question..."How much is scale?" I was prepared for that question and I told him $985. He said that would be ok with him. I was flabbergasted. Well, let's face it, he really didn't need the money and it meant more for him to do the film than making any money from it. The producer fell in love with me...the fact that I could get a name like that for such little money overwhelmed him...and me.

Steve, as a gesture of appreciation, signed over to my music publishing company the publishing rights to the music from the film. The music to the film turned out better than expected with additional recordings by jazz artists aside from our soundtrack recording.

After I started my Beverly Hills Record company, Chet Baker came to Steve Allen to borrow $10,000. Steve told him he would give him the money as a fee to record twelve of his original jazz tunes. Chet Baker agreed. Steve produced the album and as a token of appreciation gave it to me for my record company. Chet's LP was labeled *Albert's House*.

Steve was a great friend and the most caring and considerate person I had ever met. I miss our lunch meetings at his office in Burbank, always feeling proud of his relying on me for information regarding the ins and outs of the Music Business. I sure wish he was still around.

Side One

THE SWINGIN' DAGGER THEME	3:07
MELISSA	1:45
THE CAR CHASE	1:52
THE MEAT PLANT	2:19
THE FUN AND GAMES CHASE	1:05
FIRST ALLEY FLIGHT	1:40

Side Two

INGRID'S BLUES	1:51
FIGHT WITH OTTO	2:12
NUTTY KOFFMAN	1:23
THE DEATH OF KOFFMAN	1:23
A MAN CALLED DAGGER (INSTRUMENTAL VERSION)	3:01
A MAN CALLED DAGGER (VOCAL VERSION)	2:32

Music Composed by Steve Allen
Lyrics by Buddy Kaye
Vocal by Maureen Arthur
Album produced by Morris I. Diamond
Music Conducted, Arranged,
and Adapted by Ronald Stein
Publisher: Jo-Al Music, ASCAP
Director of Engineering: Val Valentin

THE MUSIC AND STEVE ALLEN

Most of the world's talented people are satisfied to enter the Hall of Fame via a single avenue. This is not the case with Steve Allen, the composer of the score for "A Man Called Dagger." He has gained recognition for many accomplishments in a variety of creative endeavors. He is, of course, not only a composer, but a TV and motion picture star, a leading comedian, a lyricist, public speaker, pianist and serious author, well-thought of by critics for the eleven books he has written.

Steve Allen has written more than 2,000 songs including such popular standards as This Could Be The Start of Something Big, Pretend You Don't See Her, South Rampart Street Parade, Picnic, Gravy Waltz and Impossible. His words and music for the NBC-TV spectacular "The Bachelor" won him a Sylvania Award. Allen, who writes an average of three songs a week, has also written the title numbers for the motion pictures "Picnic," "Houseboat," "On The Beach," "Sleeping Beauty" and "Bell, Book and Candle."

High on the roster of his musical accomplishments was his writing of words and music for the Broadway musical "Sophie," based on the life of Sophie Tucker.

A MAN CALLED DAGGER

E 4514
SE 4514

Music From The Original Sound Track

An extremely high-caliber film of international intrigue, the action-packed A Man Called Dagger pounds out one exciting scene after another like a massive trip-hammer. Producer Lewis M. Horwitz has scored an imaginative coup in commissioning many-faceted Steve Allen to compose the music for his production. A songwriter of enormous versatility and staggering output, Allen's music provides a tense accompaniment for this exciting film. Additionally, it stands on its own as music for music's sake.

Dagger (PAUL MANTEE) trails ex-Nazi scientist Karl Reiner (LEONARD STONE) from Europe to the United States while probing the international traffic of other ex-Nazis. The scent leads to Rudolph Koffman (JAN MURRAY), former SS Colonel and concentration camp commandant. Beautiful, American agent, Harper Davis (TERRY MOORE), essays the situation for Dagger. It appears Koffman owns and operates a meatpacking plant. It is suspected as a front for neo-Nazi experimental work and Dagger decides to investigate.

He visits Koffman's mistress, Ingrid (SUE ANE LANGDON), ensconced in a luxurious mansion staffed by beautiful young girls. But Ingrid is elusive and Dagger gets nowhere with his questioning until he meets up with Ingrid's masseuse, Joy (MAUREEN ARTHUR). Dagger gets his first lead from her. He must talk to Joy's friend, Erica (EILEEN O'NEILL), who is imprisoned at Koffman's plant.

That evening, Dagger invades this fortress and kidnaps Erica. But Koffman has monitored every move and is already holding Harper hostage! Defenceless against this chicanery, Dagger effects a prisoner exchange and is back at the starting gate. He forces Ingrid to reveal the secret entrance to Koffman's plant and arrives to find Joy is now being held by the power-hungry Fascist. Koffman's plan is, in fact, to capture the leaders of the Free World, brainwash them and plant small radio receivers in their teeth—thus giving him complete control over them.

The capture, brainwashing and torture of Dagger precede the violent conclusion to this exciting film. Dagger escapes and is pursued. But he finally confronts Koffman in a huge meat locker containing hundreds of hanging carcasses and kills the would-be world dictator in a vivid and unforgettable finale.

Tom Rolfe

TERRY MOORE · JAN MURRAY · SUE ANE LANGDON · PAUL MANTEE
EILEEN O'NEILL · MAUREEN ARTHUR · LEONARD STONE · MIMI DILLARD · RICHARD NG · JAMES ZAIMAN and RICHARD KIEL—KILY
RICHARD RUSH · LEWIS M HORWITZ · M. ZAFFOS ····· STEVE ALLEN ···· In METROCOLOR

MGM RECORDS

METRO-GOLDWYN-MAYER

This record has been engineered and manufactured in accordance with standards developed by the Record Industry Association of America, Inc., a copyright organization dedicated to the betterment of recorded music and fidelity.

MANUFACTURED AND DISTRIBUTED IN CANADA BY QUALITY RECORDS LIMITED
380 BIRCHMOUNT ROAD, TORONTO, ONTARIO.

COVER PRINTED IN U.S.A.

The liner notes are of the soundtrack that Steve wrote for the film.

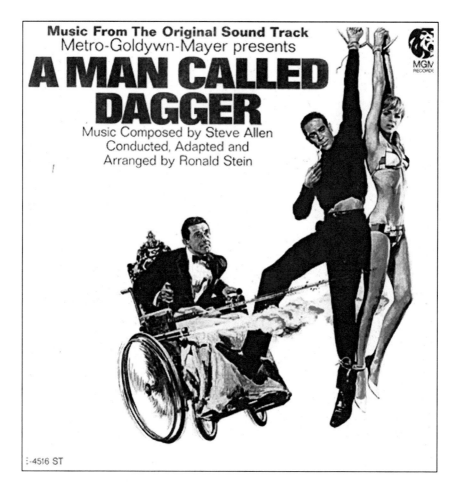

Chapter Twenty-Two
THE SMOTHERS BROTHERS

Some of my happiest days as National Promotion Director at Mercury Records were dealing with Tom and Dick Smothers. Working on eight of their albums from 1962 through 1966 was a labor of love.

Their promotion-minded team consisted of superstar managers Ken Kragen and Ken Fritz. The Smothers were never that demanding and very cooperative. They believed strongly in record promotion and made themselves available for whatever promotional activity we would concoct. At one time they were playing in Chicago (Mercury's headquarters), and our president, Irving Green, had received a request form a buddy who owned a slew of radio stations to ask The Smothers if they would do a number of station breaks. Irving didn't want to say yes or no to his acquaintance and turned the project over to me. I called Ken Kragen who said he would check it out and get back to me. Within a half hour, I got a call from Tom Smothers asking me where and when we wanted them to do the spots. I told them that we had the facilities in our office to do it at their convenience. They showed up at the office within the hour and performed the request magnificently.

Their popularity with the public increased as the years went by, particularly with the recognition they finally received for their infamous and unforgettable CBS TV *Smothers Brothers* show that ran from February, 1967 through June, 1969. They broke the barriers of first amendment rights on that show by poking fun at organized religion and the politics. Word has it that President Nixon told CBS to get rid of them. Many stars such as Dr. Spock, Joan Baez and Harry Belafonte wanted to appear on the show and get their personal licks in with anti-war or anti-draft messages. There's no question that they helmed the most controversial TV show in the history of television. They followed that show with a summer run in 1970 on ABC-TV and another five month run on NBC-TV in 1975. Those shows didn't have the "balls" as did the CBS-TV bonanza. Their efforts were finally recognized in September, 2008, during the telecast of the 60th Primetime Emmy Awards, when Tommy Smothers, who was actually the head writer of their infamous Comedy Hour, was finally awarded the 1968 Emmy for Outstanding Writing in a Comedic Series. Back in 1968, Tommy didn't want to enter his name to the list of writers that were nominated for the Emmy because of the "controversies" he felt would screw up their chances for an Emmy award...which they ultimately did win.

Other than their series of Comedy Hours, both Tom and Dick do quite well acting separately in dramatic film and TV projects. When asked about his thoughts about his brother Dick, Tom is quoted as saying "We still disagree about everything. I mean, he's more conservative politically and also is a pragmatist. He's very pragmatic and wants everything to line up and put in a box. And I'm a little bit looser." In 2003, they were awarded the George Carlin Freedom of Expression Award from the Video Software Dealers' Association; recognizing their "extraordinary comic gifts and their unfailing support of the First Amendment." They both received Honorary Doctorate Degrees from San Jose State University the same year. In 2008, they received A Lifetime Achievement Award from the Boston Comedy Festival.

A few years ago I attended a wedding in Northern California's wine country, Napa Valley. Shouldn't be a total loss I took a shot and checked the phone book for The Smother's winery, Remick Ridge Vineyards, and lo and behold I found it would be just a fifteen minute drive. It was fronted by a lovely wine and accessory store. As my wife and I entered the store, I heard "Morris?" It was Tom's wife, Marcy, who it seems, ran the store. We had a couple of tastings and I picked out a couple of bottles of Merlot—and PAID for them. Tommy was on the road that week. If he were there, I'm sure he'd at least have given me half off. Oh well, you can't win 'em all.

Which reminds me of a story that Tom tells every time we got into a discussion about religion. Tom's first marriage was to a young

Backstage in Vegas (L-R) Me, Dick and Tom Smothers, Dick Sherman who was sales manager at Mercury Records in the 60's.

lady who was Jewish...and so was the wedding ceremony. As Tom tells the story, "At the end of the ceremony, to seal the union, they put the little traditional shot glass by my feet and as directed, I crushed it...twelve stitches." Of course, it did go smoothly and no injuries were sustained.

On one of their first appearances on the *Tonight Show* on NBC, after they did a few minute routine and sat and chatted with Johnny Carson. They were thanked by Carson when he said, "it was nice having you on my show." Tom replied, "It was nice being had." I was in the green room joining the other guests in a great laugh.

As of this writing, we are approximately forty-five years later. The Smothers are as popular as they were way back when. I manage to see them a number of times a year whether it be in Vegas, L.A. or Palm Springs. We share fond memories of many road trips together.

Chapter Twenty-Three
LESLEY GORE

We read about people in the entertainment industry taking credit for some personality's fame. "Oh, if it wasn't for me, so and so would never have had the success or fame they have achieved" Well, I wouldn't go so far, but there are perhaps just a few records that I could pat myself on the back for whatever success occurred in a small way. Undoubtedly, if the talent wasn't there, no matter how many strings we have to pull to get a record played, nothing would happen.

Sixteen year old Lesley Gore's Mercury recording of "It's My Party" back in 1963 had "hit" written all over it from the get-go. As National Promotion director of the label, it wasn't a difficult task to talk my thirty-three promotion men and women around the country into getting the top radio stations in their area to play the record, particularly after they heard it. In no time at all, the requests were pouring in for Lesley to make personal appearances at record hops em-ceed by the various disc jockeys around the country. One of the first hops to submit a request for Lesley was from Jerry Sharell, my Cleveland promo guy. He wanted to know if Lesley would be available for a hop run by Chuck Dunaway, DJ and program director of WIXY in Cleveland. I told him I'd check it out and get back to him ASAP.

I got the green light from Lesley's dad, Leo, who also mentioned that when we organize tickets for the flight from Newark to Cleveland, to make sure that there's one for Lesley and one for her mother—which was understandable, Leslie being a minor.

I called the travel agent who organized the transportation and hotel for Lesley and her mother and who also notified Leo Gore as

Backstage with Lesley Gore at The Stardust in las Vegas where she starred in the Women Legends of Rock 'n Roll.

well. Leo called me immediately and said—"Morris, it's been thirty years since any of my family or I have traveled coach, and we're not about to start now. Would you please organize the proper tickets for us?" I apologized, and ordered the appropriate flight tickets, and continued the same procedure on whatever promotion I sent her on. The family was most cooperative and reasonable in their demands to be accommodated according to their lifestyle.

Lesley lived with her parents, Leo and Ronnie in a fashionable home in New Jersey, just across the George Washington Bridge, along with her younger brother, Michael, who achieved success on his own beginning with composing the score for the Broadway hit show, *Fame*, which ultimately led him to more Broadway stage show scores along with films and TV.

Lesley Gore being interviewed by DJ Hal Jackson in Palisades Park, New Jersey in 1965. L-R: Hal; ; Lesley's record producer, a young kid by the name of Quincy Jones; Lesley, Me and a friend.

One of Quincy Jones' first assignments as head of A & R for Mercury Records was to produce Lesley's first record. After going through a slew of suggested songs, Quincy decided that "It's My Party" should be the kicker in the first recording session...and it was.

Being the stage parent that he was, Leo Gore was constantly on the phone with the president of Mercury Records, Irving Green. He was not the usual parent nudge, but wanted to be kept abreast of the progress of Lesley's new hit record. After a few calls, Mr. Green suggested that all future calls go to me or/and Quincy. The boss put us totally in charge of Lesley—her recordings...what to record, when to record—when to release what record—what to promote—where to promote—the whole shebang. Leo was content with that arrangement and so were we.

Lesley's future charted hits became a labor of love—among them, "You Don't Own Me," "Judy's Turn To Cry," "Sunshine, Lollipops, and Rainbows." Lesley and I had an enviable rapport with each other. In subsequent interviews, when asked about her relationship with the record company, she would quote me when I would tell her to "have LES Gore and MOR Diamond." I'm proud to say that we still have that same (corny?) routine to this day.

I've gone to Las Vegas a number of times when Lesley headlined the "Ladies of Rock & Roll" show at The Stardust Hotel. I couldn't have been more proud if she was my own daughter. She turned out to be not just a good performer, but a wonderful entertainer. And the beat goes on!

Chapter Twenty-Four
DIZZY GILLESPIE

I always had a strong desire to attend one of the great Jazz Festivals of all time, The Monterey Jazz Fest...held, where else, in Monterey, California. Having just started as National Promo Director of Mercury, I came up with a plan that would allow me a promotional visit to the Festival.

In 1962, Dizzy Gillespie had just a couple of months earlier joined us at Mercury Records, and I was as well a comparative newcomer to the label. At one of our board meetings, I came up with the idea that we should do a national promotion job for Dizzy. I told all the brass at Mercury that Dizzy would be playing the Monterey Jazz Festival in September and suggested that we make the day after he closes, "G DAY" all over the country. I told them I would make sweat-shirts with a caricature of Dizzy, and send them to all our distributors' sales and promotion forces and everyone of them would wear the sweat shirts on that designated day after his appearance in Monterey; and that I would fly to the festival, pick him up and take him to San Francisco, where we would spend one day of visiting disc jockeys, record shops, our record distributor and his sales and promotion staff. My bosses loved the idea and gave me the green light to proceed.

I phoned Dizzy and got the green light from him as well. I told him I would come to the festival on his closing day, catch the show, and we'd drive to San Francisco, stay at the St. Francis Hotel on Union Square, where I had our travel agent make reservations for two rooms and a suite. We had about two months to put this all into motion and I must say that the sales and art department at Mercury did a yeoman's task in getting everything in gear.

I enjoyed the Festival—it was all I expected and more. Exciting hardly describes the emotion one feels when watching and listening to all the jazz greats. I was particularly taken aback by the performance of Dizzy's new pianist from Buenos Aires, Lalo Schifrin, whose talents, as we all found out, had taken him to heights that he could never imagine as a youngster in Argentina. Prophetically, Dizzy told me to look out for Lalo's future…"He's gonna make a lot of noise," said Dizzy. I got a kick out of meeting a very shy Lalo and chatting with him after the concert. He seemed so grateful for the reception he was getting in America.

Dizzy said his goodbyes to his band and gathering fans. He and his road manager got into my rented auto and we were off to San Francisco at about midnight. We arrived at the St. Francis Hotel about an hour later, and strode into the lobby to register. The desk clerk, when seeing that I had two black men with me and not recognizing Dizzy at all, denied us our rooms. It seems that the travel agent made the reservations in my name and didn't make any reference to Dizzy at all. I showed the confirmation to the clerk but to no avail. He just kept repeating that they were filled up and all sold out. I screamed and shouted and insisted that the hotel honor the reservations, but to no avail. At that point Dizzy, being the gentle sort that he was, told me not to get that excited about their refusal because he gets a lot of that when traveling around the country. To me this was strictly a race issue with the clerk and certainly not the policy of the hotel. The clerk did make a call and got us into a small hotel about two blocks away…it wasn't the St. Francis, but it was clean and comfortable. I wrote some seething letters to the management of the big hotel and received apologies in return.

The following day we were picked up by our local San Francisco promotion man to go on the tour of duty with visits to disc jockeys, press, record stores and our local distributor. Everyone, including us, was wearing the Dizzy Gillespie sweat shirt (see photo). At Mercury Records, we had thirty-three record distributors nationally, and, consequently, thirty-three record promoters. The promoters were my team and my responsibility and were all wearing the sweat shirts on that day—"G Day." We made local newspapers and sales on Dizzy's current LP zoomed to everyone's satisfaction.

Me on the right and Dizzy Gillespie along with our record distributor's promo people on a San Francisco street.

Dizzy was as charming as can be. Everyone loved him. He also had some great lines...as for example, at one of the radio stations we walked in and he told this gorgeous receptionist—"Honey, if beauty was a disease, you'd have been dead years ago." Another great line, when he spotted another beauty, "Anyone who fucks her has to have his tongue cut out."

I didn't realize it at the time, but I was told later on that the Dizzy Gillespie sweat shirt promotion with his caricature in front was the first of its kind in the Record Business...and that was in September, 1962. I didn't get any medals for that, but I did get to go to the Monterey Jazz Festival. That was the best payoff.

Chapter Twenty-Five
QUINCY JONES

Irving Green, President of Mercury Records, has been honored numerous times through the years as having been the first to hire an African American to the position of executive of not only a major company, but a major record label. During my tenure at Mercury as national promotion director, Quincy Jones was hired as our West Coast head of A & R and vice president of the company.

His first production was the signing of sixteen year old Lesley Gore to Mercury, and hit a home run right out of the batter's box by producing Lesley's first hit recording, "It's My Party" along with other hits from her first LP. Not being egotistical, but in reality, that also happened to be one of the few records in my promotional career that I can take credit for as having personally delivered a hit to the label. This was mainly achieved due to Quincy's selection of the right song. Couldn't have done it with him.

Quincy also delivered to our label the soundtrack of *The Sandpiper*, with a score written by Johnny Mandel. It also included a tune that turned out to be a great standard, "The Shadow of your Smile," written by Johnny Mandel and Paul Francis Webster. Quincy wrote and scored the soundtrack as well for *The Pawnbroker*. These were produced in the mid-60s.

If they gave out awards for Mr. Nice Guy, Quincy would win hands down and have it displayed amongst his twenty-eight Grammy Awards. Not to mention the hordes of honorariums bestowed on him thru the years. It's incredible how he spreads his talent and personality all over the world. You can find him at home one day and the next day he's off to Darfur or Beijing or Brazil. His many trips overseas are more involved with coming to their aid or getting the people around the world involved in the causes of humanitarianism.

I've been privileged to be in his company at many music industry affairs since our days at Mercury Records, and this has been a friendship that I've treasured since the early '60s at Mercury in Chicago. Our working together on the success of "It's My Party," Irving Green gave Quincy and I the opportunity to plan all of Lesley's future releases which gave the world such chart breakers as "You Don't Own Me" as well as "Sunshine, Lollypops and Rainbows."

In 1964, at a subsequent meeting of all producers and A & R personnel from all over the US that took place in Mercury's home office in Chicago, Quincy was seated next to me. When I celebrated my birthday before going into the Air Force as flight radio operator in 1942, I was still working for the Tommy Dorsey Orchestra as assistant manager. I received many gifts from the guys in the band that were given to me mainly because I was going into the service, and also because it was my birthday. Legendary trumpeter, Ziggy Elman, gave me a beautiful set of matching cuff links and tie clip. They were emblazoned with musical notes. I don't read music and it never occurred to me to ask anyone what the notes were. At the board meeting, I was wearing them in my cuffed shirt when Quincy lifted my arm and started singing the notes on my cuff link, "I Love You, Truly," which were what the notes in my cuff links were saying to me all those years without me realizing the treasure.

I wish I knew about those notes while Ziggy was alive so I could plant a big kiss on his Jewish face.

Lesley Gore and I attended a one-on-one interview, subject matter was Quincy, and was sponsored by the Recording Academy at the Skirball Center and attended by a few hundred other fans. Aside from the interview, the gathering also served the purpose of a book-signing session for "Q" (Quincy) on the occasion of the release of his new book called—Q. He inscribed in the book "to my family, Morris and Elena, Love you forever Q." Needless to say, I treasure it.

Quincy lives on being recognized as an icon in an industry that doesn't grant that title to too many people. In the case of Quincy Jones, the word 'icon' fits like a glove.

The good looking dude is Quincy Jones pointing his finger to show one and all that Morris Diamond is alive and well. (one out two ain't bad).

Chapter Twenty-Six
JOHNNY MATHIS

I jumped with joy when Irving Green, President of Mercury Records, announced at our A & R meeting in the early '60s that we acquired Johnny Mathis to record for us.

I had heard through the years about his notorious manager, Helen Noga, who was tough and took no BS from anyone. She was notorious in the sense that when you chatted with Helen, her descriptive conversation could make a truck driver blush; if you get my drift. She was tough in the sense that if you didn't do as she asked or suggested, she'd let you know about it in no uncertain terms. She was almost always right, however—in her own way.

Having managed Johnny since the days when he appeared at The Black Hawk Club in San Francisco as far back as 1955, Helen, her husband John and their daughter Beverly, hi-tailed it to Beverly Hills where they bought a beautiful home on the corner of Sunset and Elm. At this point, Johnny was well on his way to become the superstar he is today. A few of us at Mercury had great fun when Johnny came to Chicago for a club date or concert. Being the athlete that he was before he became famous, having excelled in track and field as a high jumper and hurdler at San Francisco's George Washington High School along with earning four athletic letters on the school's basketball team, he took advantage of those of us at Mercury Records who came from The Bronx by getting us out to a local Chicago school yard to play a little basketball.

Speaking of the Nogas' beautiful home in Beverly Hills, when I left Mercury and moved to L.A., I was in touch with the Nogas. Helen asked if I played tennis. I told her I did and she offered me the use of her tennis court anytime I wanted to have a game there

Johnny Mathis threw the basketball towards the hoop and he and I never saw it come down. What an athelete! This was in a Chicago schoolyard. In the mid-sixties.

with my friends...except with one admonition...that I must get off the court should composer Paul Francis Webster show up to use the court... "Even if you're in the middle of a serve...quit." It actually happened a couple of times, but always a very friendly situation.

The basketball "players" along with myself from The Bronx were Dick Sherman, Mercury's Sales manager; Alan Mink, head of promotion for our subsidiary label, Smash Records; and that label's head honcho, Charlie Fach...he wasn't from The Bronx, but he was one of us anyway. We'd go out and shoot baskets and play a little basketball...which, after a few minutes of play felt like touch football. Of course, Johnny was the best of all of us...but we learned from him...good sportsmanship and that he was one of "the guys" at the label.

The good looking guy, Johnny Mathis, and me at an industry function.

For most of Johnny's life, he recorded for Columbia Records, with the exception that he joined Mercury Records in 1963 and gave us ten albums from then on until he left to go back to Columbia in 1967. He was most cooperative promotionally and we fully supported all of his engagements by making sure that they were well covered by our local distributor's promo domos.

He was most cooperative in the sense that you didn't have to ask him twice to make a phone call to a disc jockey, distributor sales-man or one of our field promotion men. We all gave him our best shot in trying to make his stay at Mercury Records as successful as had been with Columbia—and he worked closely with us to help us achieve that aim.

Chapter Twenty-Seven
SHELBY SINGLETON

When one talks and recalls "the good old days in Nashville," a must is The Ryman Theatre, the great American treasure—home of the Grand Ole Opry and many nationally radio broadcast and television shows. Another national treasure that's a must was Shelby Singleton. I think it would be safe to say that a good portion of the stars that appeared on Grand Ole Opry were there because Shelby was single handedly responsible for the success that put them there.

When I came on board at Mercury Records in 1962, Shelby was by then a full fledged record producer and head of its "Country and Western" division in Nashville. His career with Mercury began as record promoter while living in Shreveport, Louisiana for the local branch of Mercury Records in 1958. He worked his way up the proverbial ladder and as producer, brought home such great artists as Ray Stevens, LeRoy Van Dyke, Brook Benton, Roger Miller and Jerry Lee Lewis.

He was a joy to work with. His name alone would pave the way for our promotional people to plug the newer acts that he produced. His sense of humor was always a huge plus in making everyone feel comfortable in his company. At one point, we had a national meeting in the Mercury Records boardroom in Chicago. All A & R men, sales managers, distributor heads, our regional promo men were in attendance. We took a dinner break the first day and Mercury's president, Irv Green, announced that we all go to dinner at The Shanghai Restaurant on State Street, just around the corner from our offices.

Shelby Singleton bending over my right shoulder to teach me how to play the guitar. The country singer in front of me trying to take the guitar away from me is Faron Young. Taken on the stage of the Ryman Theatre, home of the Grand Ole Opry in Nashville.

In the restaurant, I was pleased to see Shelby was sitting on my right. I don't really believe that he had ever been to a Chinese restaurant. Mr. Green did the ordering. Opening with spare ribs and wonton soup was enjoyed by all. Then everyone was served a huge combination plate—shrimp with lobster sauce, lemon chicken, fried rice, beef lo mein. Shelby looked at his dish and proclaimed to all, "Hey, this looks like it's already been et."

We both left Mercury Records in 1966. He started his own companies, SSS International and Plantation Records. His first hit out of the batters box was "Harper Valley PTA," which enabled him to be involved with the TV show follow-up as well. A year later he purchased legendary Sun Records, including its rock and roll catalog and merchandising which included names as Elvis, Cash, Jennings, etc.

For many years I've attended the super international music conference, MIDEM, in Cannes. In attendance at all times was Shelby, his wife Mary, his brother and partner, John and his wife

Nashville's legend record producer, Shelby Singleton and me at his 75th birthday party in Nashville in 2008.

Mary…and one year Shelby and Mary brought their son, Stuart. We always had time for each other at the convention and often times made plans for staying in Southern France for another few days after the conference to bum around together. And guess what was one of Shelby's favorite restaurants…a Chinese restaurant…in Cannes.

My wife gave me an "once-in-a-lifetime" birthday party a few years back at The Friar's Club in Beverly Hills. Among the cherished guests were The Singletons; Shelby, Mary and little Stuart; brother John and Mary. Instead of bringing 8x10 enlargements of photos that he had, he made huge posters of photos that showed Shelby and me with many of our top-drawer Country acts on stage at The Ryman Theatre, home of The Grand Ole Opry in Nashville. The posters were posted all over the walls of The Friar's Club to everyone's delight—especially mine.

I flew to Nashville for Shelby's 75th birthday bash in December 2006, and I cherish the time I spent with him at this heavily attended party at the local AFM building, but also at his home the next couple of days. Shelby left us on October 7, 2009.

He was truly one of the few music industry associates that I loved like a brother.

Chapter Twenty-Eight
"BARBARA ANN"

Living in The Bronx as a teenager and as a rather young man had its advantages if music is imbedded in one's soul. And it is in mine.

I don't recall how it happened, but in the late fifties I found myself hanging around Cousins Record Store on Fordham Road, not too far from where I lived in The Bronx. Proprietor was a delightful gent by the name of Lou Chicchetti. The Italian section of The Bronx was Arthur Avenue; also not too far from Cousins Record Store, but in a different direction than from where I lived.

We hit it off nicely, both having the same feeling for music of all genres. Lou's store was also a hangout for young pop singers and doo-woppers, mostly from the Arthur Avenue section.

Newly formed vocal groups hung out and rehearsed on street corners and at the store...such as, Dion DiMucci and the Belmonts, The Tremonts and The Regents. Lou and I nurtured them and I tried creating interest on their behalf from different record companies. In '58, Laurie Records beat us to the punch by signing Dion and the Belmonts (named after Belmont Avenue in The Bronx) and their monster hit of "I Wonder Why."

I had no luck in trying to place the demos of The Tremonts (another street in The Bronx).

In 1961, Lou and I decided to place our money where our collective mouths were and take The Regents into a recording studio at 729 7th Avenue in Manhattan and produce a couple of sides. One of the tunes was "Barbara Ann," written by Freddie Fassert, whose brother, Chuck, was one of the vocal group.

Number one on the top 100 Chart in 1965, a tune that I published, "Barbara Ann"

After the session, I took a demo home and played it for my thirteen-year-old daughter, JoAnne, who immediately declared it a hit record. The following day I took it to my boss, Bob Thiele (he and Steve Allen owned Hanover-Signature Records, of which, at the time, I was National Sales and promotion manager). I didn't expect him to like or do anything with it, mainly because this type of music wasn't his bag. Bob was unquestionably, one of the best minds in jazz. I felt it was my obligation to at least play it for him and get his thoughts.

Our company had some financial difficulties and Bob had made a deal with Roulette Records owner, Morris Levy, to bail us out; and because we were "in bed" with Levy, we also had office space available to us at Levy's label, Roulette Records. After listening to the demo of Barbara Ann, Bob liked it but rightfully felt that it wasn't right for our label, but suggested that we play the demo for Levy. Which we did. He loved it.

I was excited until I found out later that the rumors on the street were that if you made a deal with Morris Levy, not getting paid your royalties on time or at all was a strong possibility. Morris was an affable guy and my partner Lou and I felt that he was anxious about our production and he would make it a priority to service our recording promotionally and marketing-wise. He paid us an advance of $500, which just about covered the cost of our record session.

By sheer coincidence, Levy's lawyer was also my lawyer, Walter Hofer. Two years prior, Walter was plugging records in New York while attending law school. We buddied around together. I took him on my rounds of the disc jockeys and radio stations from time to time. We played poker once a week. I attended his two marriages. At the same time he was traveling to Europe every opportunity he had and locked himself in with The Beatles manager, Brian Epstein. When he finally got his law degree, he was representing The Beatles in their early days of their invasion of the United States. When Walter opened his first office on Broadway and 53rd Street, I was up there helping him erect the metal shelves in his filing cabinets. I mention all of this for a reason as you will read later on in this chapter.

He had nothing to do with the actual negotiations involved in the licensing of the master recording to Roulette. I did that one-on-one with Levy. Now the record is released on a Roulette subsidiary label, Gee Records and doing quite well. Hitting radio charts all over the US and showing up on the music trade charts as well— Billboard, Record World and Cashbox. This was in 1961. Now I was approached for Lou and me to give Gee Records the rights to license the record and song internationally. We were 50/50 partners on the music publishing. We did that and were given another $500 advance for foreign rights.

After about four months of anxiety, I got a call to pop in on Walter Hofer's office on W 57th Street. He gave me a check from Roulette Records for five grand. No statement, just a check. I asked about the statement. His reply was that I should be grateful to get the check, and that is how my partner and I would be compensated from time to time. I did get a few checks thereafter…again with no statement.

Early in 1962, I accepted the job as National Promotion Director of Mercury Records in Chicago. In 1965 I received a call from a friend who was involved in the record promotion department at Capitol Records in Hollywood. Knowing that Lou and I owned the music publishing, he called to tell me that The Beach Boys covered "Barbara Ann" and they were going all out on a heavy promotion drive to bring the record home. I was thrilled and immediately put my thinking cap on.

I called Al Peckover, the accountant at Roulette Records in New York, and without tipping my hat about the Beach Boys record, I asked for all of my rights to the recording of "Barbara Ann" be returned to me. He said that would not be possible because we have an agreement. I came back with the simple fact that in the four years Roulette has had international rights we were never given a statement, consequently breaching the basic agreement that we had. I got nowhere with him.

Now I called my old friend, Walter Hofer, and asked him, as my lawyer, to get me my record rights back from Morris Levy and Roulette Records, and I told him why…again not telling him about the new Beach Boys version. He said he would call me back. He called me back to tell me that in order for me to get the song back, I would have to sue all the licensees all over the world. I told him "baloney." My only licensee is Roulette Records and they breached their agreement by not giving me statements through the years. He flatly told me that I was not getting my song back. This was my close personal friend who I nurtured in the record business basically telling me that his total allegiance was with Morris Levy. I tried getting other attorneys involved and was flatly refused because of fear. They just didn't want to oppose Morris Levy.

The Beach Boys record of "Barbara Ann" went number one on the trade charts and was a smash worldwide.

I left Mercury Records in 1966 and moved to Los Angeles. I tried to get attorneys in L.A. and Beverly Hills to take over the case of suing Morris Levy, but to no avail. I still owned 50% of the song, and was making fairly decent dollars on domestic licenses.

I had occasion to go to Europe to work on the music of *Chitty Chitty Bang Bang* a few times in 1968. While in various countries, I checked out the foreign licensees that represented Roulette and Gee Records. I was beside myself. Everyone was very cooperative, but their agreements were with Levy and couldn't help me. But I was supplied with enough information to know that my share of foreign income paid to Roulette should have been about $100,000. When I returned to the States, I phoned Hofer. His reply was that my foreign income was more in the area of approximately $140,000 and there was nothing he could or would do for me.

Now I was ready to sell my 50% share of the copyright. I attended the NARM (National Associate of Record Merchandisers) convention in Miami in 1976. I bumped into Morris Levy and asked if he would buy my half of the publishing. He offered me $5,000. I told him that Murray Deutsch, another music publisher, offered me $10,000. He walked away.

That evening I got into a poker game with a bunch of record promoters from around the country. We all knew each other well. Red Schwartz, who was promotion man for Roulette Records, came over to me and suggested that I "back off Morris Levy." I asked what that meant, and he repeated the sentence again. Obviously I must have upset Morris about our earlier conversation asking him to buy my half of the song.

A year later, 1977, the same convention was in L.A. at the Century Plaza Hotel. In the lobby at lunchtime, I was approached by Phil Kahl, who ran the music publishing operations for Morris Levy. He told me that he's ready to buy my half of Barbara Ann...I said, "Keep talking!" He offered me $15,000. I told him he's out of the ball park. He kept haggling and we settled for $25,000 green. We met in the lobby again in the evening. He took me up to Morris Levy's suite and we sealed the deal. Morris paid me $5,000 cash on the spot; flew me to New York two weeks later all expenses paid, and put me up at the Park Lane Hotel, he paid me the balance of the deal, we signed the papers, and that ended my share of ownership of Barbara Ann. I still retained the music publishing of a number of other tunes from the original Regents' album.

Many of my friends have asked me through the years if I ever had regrets about selling the song. My answer was simple. As long as

Morris Levy had possession of the foreign rights, there was no way I would ever get a good count. Also there was no way that I could get another music publisher to buy my half of the song as long as Morris Levy was involved. I truly never had regrets. Why?

I took the money that I received from Morris and used it as a down payment for a new home in Sherman Oaks. The home cost me $150,000. I sold the home twenty-five years later for $1,250,000 when the real estate market was booming. I feel as though I've been well compensated for all my trouble through the years with "Barbara Ann."

Chapter Twenty-Nine
NORM CROSBY

Another regular comedian at our daily lunches was Norm Crosby. For many years, he was a Vegas favorite as well as holding the record for the most appearances by a comedian on the *Ed Sullivan Show*. One thing about Norm, he's always working.

Since 1983, he had been co-host of the Jerry Lewis yearly MDA Labor Day weekend telethon. He performs many times a year on cruises and when he returns, he is not bashful to tell all at our tables at lunch that he "killed them." He never had a bad show. It's possible—but I don't know.

I was working with a producer in Palm Springs, Bob Alexander. He was putting together two pilot TV shows and asked me to be his music supervisor, which I did. I also consulted Bob in bringing him talent for the show.

One of the shows was called *The Garlic Roast* that was to roast celebrities. The panel on the dais were all look and sound-a-likes of the likes of Jack Benny, George Burns, Lucille Ball, Dean Martin, etc. On our first show, the honoree to be roasted was actually Mickey Rooney. I had suggested Norm Crosby as the host. Bob liked the idea and hired him. I got him the job. After it was all over, I had asked him for my commission, but all he would talk about was his manager and "that's who gets his commission." I argued that it was I that got him the gig, not his manager. I never got a cup of coffee for my efforts. I never really held it against him because we've been good friends for many years.

Conversely, the other TV show was sort of a Dick Clark *American Bandstand*-type show called *The Beat Goes On*, and I was able to get famed disc jockey and game show host, Wink Martindale to host

L-R: Me, Joanie Crosby, Marta Lee (George Schlatter's Executive Assistant), Norm Crosby.

the show. I never said a word to Wink about the commission; however, good friend that he is, a few days after the filming, there was a check in the mail from Wink and Sandy Martindale. A class act.

One nice thing about Norm Crosby is that he lends his celebrity to charity golf tournaments and he will share a souvenir cap or tee shirt that he would get in his giveaway gift bag to his friends, me included. He generally wears something—a shirt, a jacket, a cap or some giveaway bearing the name of the various golf tournaments that he attends. I once told him "Thank G-d for golf tournaments, you wouldn't have a thing to wear." He took it in good stride.

Here we are in 2011 and Norm is still hanging in there working his cruises, along with a casino and club date here and there.

Chapter Thirty
SHECKY GREENE

The first comedian that I ever befriended was Shecky Greene, probably the funniest and most successful to play Las Vegas and successful to the extent that he is now legendary.

This goes back to the early '60s when I moved to Chicago to head Mercury Records' promotion staff. We actually met in Vegas, and when, in conversation we both realized we're from Chicago, that started the beginning of a beautiful friendship.

When he was not traveling, we met every Saturday for breakfast at Eli's Deli off Rush Street. I had not brought my family to Chicago just yet from The Bronx, so it was a nice respite for me and pleasant company to start a weekend with.

Fast forward about ten years and now we're all living in and around Beverly Hills. I got to schmooz with a bunch of guys at a daily lunch that you can read about in this book somewhere in a chapter titled "Caffe Roma." Shecky was one of the guys, always making his presence known by singing something funny on his way to our table...but entertaining to all the diners as well.

The name "Shecky" has been synonymous in almost anyone's description of Las Vegas. I think that along with Keely Smith and Louis Prima, Shecky's show was one of the hottest tickets in Vegas, and here we are in 2011, and he still plays Vegas to capacity crowds three or four times a year.

No matter what restaurant you go to, if Shecky's one of the diners, you can bet your bottom dollar that he's gonna make his presence known by belting a parody or two to the other diners.

He's mellowed in recent years having given up his going to the track and cutting down totally on his intake of the hard stuff. All

L-R: VP of music for Warner Brothers Films, Gary leMel, Shecky Greene, Me, Jerry Sharell, CEO/President of Society of Singers.

this mainly due to his third wife, Marie, daughter of the late-great tenor-sax man, Vido Musso. Marie, to my thinking, was the only wife that really cares about his personal life as opposed to his other two ex-wives who were more concerned about his professional life and their existence.

To me, one of Shecky's funniest routines that he tells of himself to his audience is about the time he was arrested for being very drunk and making a nuisance of himself in the casino after his show.

He tells of being taken to the police station and the officer advised him that he could make one phone call, who would he like to call. "The liquor store" was his brilliant and hilarious reply.

One of my clients in the late '80s was a record company in Hamburg, Germany; Teldec Records. I was hired as their American A & R man. It was a one year deal that ended with the purchase of the company by Warner Brothers Records in Europe. I was able to satisfy their needs when I brought them La Toya Jackson, among others, as new recording artists.

I coordinated my activities with Sherman Heinig, who was head of A & R for the label. He later moved to L.A. and we became partners in a few ventures. The owner of Teldec was a lovely man, Jack Dimenstein, whose wife, Sarah, was also very involved in the activities of the company. They lived in Zurich.

On one of my European trips, my wife, Elena, and I decided to visit Zurich. As requested by the Dimensteins, whenever we were in town, give them a call...which we did. They insisted that their driver pick us up at our hotel and take us to a restaurant to have dinner with them...which we did.

They asked a couple of their friends who were sitting nearby to join us. The wife of their friends mentioned to me that she wanted to give her husband a birthday party in a few months and would I know a "famous comedian" who would fly to Zurich and perform for a half hour at the party in a restaurant. I mentioned Shecky as a good possibility. She was excited at the thought.

Her offer was almost unbelievable. She would fly Shecky and his wife to Zurich first class on the Concorde, pay him a fee of $75,000, and give him their driver and limo to spend a week in and around Zurich. I felt for sure that this was an offer you can't refuse. I told her I'll be back in L.A. in a couple of days and I'll check it out for her and let her know. She wrote out a check made out to me for $5,000 in case I had to pay some money in front for the booking.

Three days later I phoned Shecky. He agreed that the offer was tough to refuse...However, he hadn't worked in awhile and was doing double duty with his shrink. He also told me that in two weeks he will be doing his first club date in a long time in San Francisco and would phone me that night after work and advise me as to whether it would be wise to accept our offer. Shecky called me the night after his performance..."Moishe, it ain't gonna work." He wouldn't elaborate except to say that he was not comfortable working that night not having worked in a long while. He felt he wasn't ready and wouldn't want to embarrass my friends in Zurich, and took a pass.

I phoned Dick Alen at William Morris Agency and he put a hold on Red Buttons as a replacement. The client in Zurich had her heart set on Shecky and thanked me for my help and cancelled her thoughts about an American comedian for her party. I told her that I would return her $5,000 deposit fee. She asked me to keep it for my trouble.

That was in the '80s, and here we are thirty years later and Shecky is back on stage in Vegas packing them in…as I mentioned earlier.

Chapter Thirty-One
RODNEY DANGERFIELD

Next we have the late great Rodney Dangerfield. I write elsewhere in this book about his infamous bad habit of unbuttoning his shirt and unzipping his fly in restaurants. Couldn't care less who, where or when; he wanted his comfort. In most cases he got it, then again, in some cases he was asked to zip up or get out.

He frequented our Caffe Roma lunch bunch in Beverly Hills, and one day we all decided to drive up to Oxnard for a day of fun in the sun, Rodney included. One of our gang had clout with the Embassy Suites Hotel Mandalay Beach Resort. He made a call and we were okay'd for a complimentary two bedroom suite for the day as long as they were assured that Rodney will be on the premises.

There were eight of us and we drove up from L.A. in two cars. Film producer, Dick Stenta, was the designated driver for Rodney, me, and owner of the late La Cage Aux Folles L.A. nightclub, Murray Drezner. It was a fun trip.

We arrived at the resort and not needing to check in at all, we were escorted to our lovely suite. It wasn't but a few minutes later that the second car with the other guys showed up. We sat around, admiring the beautiful suite, and we can't find Rodney. Just then, Rodney appeared from one of the bedrooms...stark naked. No robe, no towel to cover his beautiful (?) body. We're throwing lines at him like, "Hey, we came here to enjoy the sights...but this?" and "what are you so proud of"? He couldn't care less. We were somewhat relieved when he put on a pair of pants so we could go down to the beach and hang out...and he hung out...er...literally and figuratively.

Living the good life in Oxnard, L-R: Me, Rodney Dangerfield, John Huddy, General manager of KADY-TV in Oxnard, CA.

That's the way Rodney was. If you visited him at his suite on top of the Beverly Hilton Hotel in Beverly Hills, he would sit around without a stitch of clothes...unless, of course, if there was a lady present, he would wear a robe...that would inadvertently open....I couldn't find anything for him to be proud of...then again, I didn't look too closely!

At one time, a very dear friend, Flo Levy, who was an agent/ manager at the time, asked me to set up an appointment for her to have a meeting with Rodney. There was no problem at all and the meeting was in Rodney's suite at the Beverly Hilton Hotel.

Sure enough, Rodney greeted her at the door wearing his robe, but not totally closed (the robe, not the door). "He had no ulterior motive," Flo recalled, "but he looked like he was ready for action but was actually very sweet and businesslike."

On his 70th birthday, his wife, Joan, decided to give him a birthday party in the party room of their new residence on Wilshire Boulevard. Believe it or not, he was shy about personal affairs, and the bets going around the packed birthday room were that he wouldn't show. But he surprised everyone and did show and he spent most of the evening in a corner with his old friend, and new star on the horizon, Jim Carrey. He gave most of us a red tie with his signature theme printed on it. "I Get No Respect." A fun evening was had by all.

Later that year, Dick Stenta and his family invited a few friends to his home for Christmas Dinner—including my wife and I and Rodney. It was lovely because he behaved as though he was at home with his own family. It was a different Rodney that evening. He was at peace with himself.

We lost Rodney in October, 2004 at the age of 83.

Chapter Thirty-Two
OLIVIA NEWTON-JOHN

In the early '70s, when Artie Mogull was head of A&R at MCA records, one of his pet projects was Olivia Newton-John. Artie and I had been very close since his early days in the music business in 1949 as bandboy for the Tommy Dorsey Orchestra; a job I had in 1941. Consequently, Artie and I were invited to many of the same house parties and events that included Olivia as well. We all became fast friends.

When I shelved my Beverly Hills Records Label in 1974, Artie was out on his own. He started a production company and I went to work for him. In those days we spent much social time with Olivia and her boy friend/manager, Lee Kramer. For a long while, we were on Olivia's "A" list, and after that we found ourselves advanced to her "family" list. Olivia would return from a tour, call my wife and invite us to a dinner that Saturday night at her home in Malibu because "Mum's coming in from Australia."

Shortly after the first of January in 1975, Olivia called the office to say hello to Artie and myself. I was at home and not feeling well and Artie told her so when she asked about me. She was calling from Acapulco and asked Artie to put me on a plane to Acapulco, where she had rented a home for a few weeks at the famous Las Brisas resort. One of the best weeks of my life. She had about eight of her closest friends there from England and Los Angeles. One evening, I was made guest of honor at a dinner at the very elegant Bellavista restaurant. Olivia made me feel special.

We stopped in Mexico City on the way back to Los Angeles so Olivia could renew her visitation visa.

Olivia Newton-John and me on holiday in Acapulco. It doesn't get any better than this.

A few months later, Olivia asked Artie if she could borrow me for a week or two to go on a mission for her. It seems that she was seriously intent on dissolving her relationships with her accountant and attorneys in London and asked if I would go there to pick up all paperwork, agreements, etc. and drop them off to her new attorney in New York City on the trip home. I was told to be very aggressive and not to leave London until the mission was accomplished.

I flew first class to London round trip, a suite at the Inn on the Park hotel, and a credit card. What's not to like! I arrived in London on a Friday morning and after checking into the hotel, I scooted over to my first destination—the accountant's office. I was told on arrival that their basement had been flooded from heavy rains and most of the paperwork that I was to pick up was waterlogged and might take a few days to dry off. I told them that it was ok with me, and that I brought a couple of books with me and that I would be very comfortable in their reception room for however long it would take for them to accommodate Olivia's request. The same conversation took place at the lawyer's office later that day.

That afternoon, both the accountant and lawyer phoned to tell me that they have the paperwork ready for me to pick up. Mission accomplished the first day of my arrival in London. I phoned Olivia's attorney in New York City and he suggested I arrive on New York on Monday and he will see me on Tuesday morning at which time I would turn over all the documents that I secured in London. It was a lovely weekend in London and with a one-day stopover in New York City; I wended my way back home to Los Angeles.

Olivia phoned me a day after my return to thank me, and told me that she will compensate me for the trip. I told her not to because I was on Artie's payroll and had myself a lovely weekend in London and then New York. She wouldn't hear of it and two days later I received a generous check from Olivia for my trouble. What a way to go!

A few weeks later came the Grammy Awards and I was invited by Olivia to attend along with her boyfriend, Lee. We sat in the first row. Olivia received an armful of awards. Every time she returned to her seat she would plop the Grammy on my lap—a few friends who had watched the show on TV, remarked that I looked a bit dazed.

In the mid-70s, Olivia was receiving crank letters brought directly to her mailbox at home in Malibu. The police were notified and assigned Neil Spotts, a detective, to handle the matter. Neil, a good looking dude and very sociable, became very friendly with Olivia's sister, Rona. That went on for a few months. When he returned to duty, Neil and I still remained friends. I became part of his weekly poker game that included FBI, and other friends of his in the entertainment industry. Neil, when he retired from the force, was hired by Hugh Hefner as his head of security. Neil would travel to all parts of the world wherever there was a problem at a Playboy Club. He also was able to put me on the invite list for many of Hugh Hefner's parties at the Playboy Mansion. He is now retired.

In years to come, Olivia got herself a new manager and for whatever reason, she and her boyfriend/manager, Lee Kramer, split. At the same time, whether it was by suggestion from her new manager or her own decisions, she cut down on her entourage. There were no more invites for parties or phone calls just to say hello. I would see her every once in awhile at a screening or an industry party and she would be her usual cordial self with a hug and a kiss and "say hi to Elena," my wife.

Both Olivia Newton-John and I were honored to have our images on display at the Palm Restaurant in Hollywood.

Olivia was a joy to have as a friend because she appreciated friendship and loyalty, but her life these days has been obsessed with her battle with cancer and raising funds for all sorts of cancer research which I thoroughly understand and applaud.

Being on Olivia's "A" list for the years that we were close, was a joy. Not only because it was Olivia, but associating with her and her choice of friends made life more pleasurable.

Chapter Thirty-Three
JACKIE VERNON

I called Jackie "the shicker with the clicker." If you don't know what "shicker" means, ask the nearest staggering Jew with a bottle of Manischevitz wine in his hand. The clicker, of course was Jackie's stand-up comedy mainstay. Clicking his way with imaginary slides…i.e. "and here we have a picture of this monstrous bear entering our campsite—click—and here we have the bear coming towards me and my camera—click—and here I am taking a picture from inside the bear's mouth—click" and stuff like that.

I signed Jackie to my Beverly Hills Records label in 1972 and we recorded a cast comedy album live in front of an industry filled audience. It was quite successful. We did get great airplay around the country. I dared call the album *Sex is NOT Hazardous To Your Health*. We had a very impressive cast: Tom Bosley, (TVs *Happy Days*), Marian Mercer and Louisa Moritz, wonderful and funny TV, film and stage actors.

Jackie's humor delivery was different from most of the stand-up comedians…it was almost like a slow drawl, but very effective.

As I mentioned, we got a lot of attention from the disc jockeys around the country. I had a situation that was about as close to a day in hell that I can ever remember. Let me tell you about it.

I got a call from my record distributor's promotion man in Seattle. One of the big personality DJs was moving on to greener pastures…(in that case, maybe a job as weatherman in Walla Walla). All the record distributors in Seattle decided to give this DJ a great send-off with an eventful affair with dinner and a show. Would I be able to get Jackie to come up for a day or so and do maybe ten minutes at the "gala." I asked Jackie and he agreed…providing they provide the

starring

Jackie Vernon

also starring

Tom Bosley
Marian Mercer
Louisa Moritz

STE

The Jackie Vernon comedy album on my label, Beverly Hills Records, Inc.

transportation from L.A. to Seattle and also a couple of rooms at the "swank" hotel that was hosting the send-off. All was agreed on and now we're set to go to Seattle. This is where the fun…or misery…began.

On the day of the affair, we had a lunch flight from Burbank to Seattle. I called Jackie to tell him I would pick him up at noon as we have a 2 p.m. flight and to be ready. He said ok. He lived on Rossmore Avenue which is the fancy shmancy street that runs from Melrose on South but is the extension of Vine Street to the North. I pulled up in front of his beautiful home and found he wasn't quite ready. "Just a couple of minutes" he yelled down. His couple of minutes in this particular situation wasn't as long as I dreaded it might be. We went down to my car. I got a parking ticket in front of his house. I expressed my indignation loudly. All he drawled was "you gotta read the signs…you can't park here after 12 p.m." Now he tells me. Ok, that was #1.

Now we're on our way to Burbank Airport. We arrive. I let him off at the main entrance and told him to wait inside with the little luggage we had while I go park the car. After parking, I entered the airport and I couldn't find him...until I got to the little lunch counter. There he was eating a chicken dinner...for lunch. I said "I told you it's a lunch flight." All he said was, "Sit down I'll buy you lunch." I paid the check and dragged him away at his displeasure by telling him that I'm gonna cancel this trip if he was going to carry on like this with his voracious appetite. This was #2. As it was, he made up for missing most of the lunch that I paid for by having a double lunch on the plane.

Now we land in Seattle and are met by my local promo rep who had no idea how heavy (fat?) Jackie was. He comes to pick us up in a Volkswagen to the bargain. Now we have to wait while the promotion man empties his back seat which was loaded with tons of boxes of LPs. How he managed to put all that garbage in his trunk mystified me...along with our baggage. We drive out of the airport and on to a freeway and we get a flat tire. It didn't take long for my record promoter and me to change the tire...what took longer than anticipated was getting all the boxes of LPs and our luggage in and out of the trunk to get to the spare tire. Of course, I sat in the back seat accompanied by more LPs and posters. There we have #3.

Now we're riding along the shore where all the fish stands and restaurants are begging us to stop so Jackie Vernon can refill his tank. Sure enough he requested a fast little shrimp cocktail. Again, I tried to reason with him in a motherly way with the warning that we'll be at the dinner within one and a half hours. He insisted and we had a fifteen minute fish stop and he finished his shrimp, mussels and clams in the car.

Hello, # 4.

Next we get to the hotel which was a classy joint. I went inside to check in. I turn around and I don't see Vernon...and he's not too difficult to notice. I found him at the candy counter with two of each—Mounds, Baby Ruth, Hershey Bars, and Snickers...oh, also a couple of packs of M&Ms. I gave him a dirty look and he replied by asking me to give the attendant my room number to charge all the goodies. Aha...#5.

I called his room at 6 p.m., our scheduled time to attend the affair. He uttered that he wasn't feeling well but was hungry enough for dinner. G-d bless him—I don't know where he puts it...but you can tell where at a glance. We took our seats in the ballroom and were asked by the emcee of the affair if Jackie would want to deliver his presentation early in the show or later on. I suggested later on, after he ate. Luckily I did, because after the first course of a shrimp cocktail, he said that he wasn't feeling too good. I asked our host if there was a doctor in the house and fortunately, there was. The doctor took Jackie into the men's room and forced him to give back everything he ate that day. And voila, Jackie felt better and delivered a nice tribute to the honored disc jockey. I'm not gonna give this a number.

Oddly enough, the following day everything went smoothly. Our trip to the airport, and then on to Burbank airport, was effortless...until I went to get my car in the Burbank Airport garage and found the right front fender of my Mercedes was bashed in. That was #6.

Yes, this was a trip from hell and one I shant forget, but basically, Jackie was a very sweet, cooperative guy. Not half as dull as he pretends to be on stage. We lost Jackie on November 10, 1987 at age 63.

Chapter Thirty-Four
STEVE TYRELL

One of the fastest rising performers in popularity that graced the stages and screens of the United States and Europe. The gravel voiced vocalist, who can bring to mind the voices of Louie Armstrong and Ray Charles singing the same song at the same time.

Our relationship had gone way back to the days when he was a young Texan who saw the light of day in 1959, and was then promoting records for Scepter Records, owned by Florence Greenberg. His talents caught the eye of Burt Bacharach and Hal David, two of the most prolific songwriters this side of Lieber and Stoller. He ultimately became a record producer and film music supervisor as well.

While serving as music supervisor for the Steve Martin hit flick, *Father of the Bride* in 1991, Steve suggested to the director that a song called *The Way You Look Tonight* would look and sound good at a certain part of the picture, and proceeded to demonstrate the song. The director flipped, not only at the thought of using the song, but also Steve's rendition, and told Steve that he wanted him to do the vocal in the film and also, for the same nickel, do the vocal on "My Girl"…another of Steve's thoughts for the film.

That was the beginning of Steve Tyrell's career as a recording artist and world-wide acceptance as a first class TV & concert performer.

Through the years, Steve had his share of managers and agents. I partnered with Kenny Fritz in managing Steve for a year. It was a blast. It pretty much was the beginning of a beautiful friendship. Our association with Steve and The William Morris Agency proved beneficial in many ways, paving the way for Steve's acceptance as a recording artist and performer. I enjoyed his performing well enough to want to attend every gig we were involved in.

Steve Tyrell making google eyes at Keely Smith who was with me at Wink Martindale's Star dedication on Hollywood Boulevard.

Ken Fritz got very involved with Columbia Records, Steve's label, and was able to spread the gospel about Steve Tyrell to a number of Columbia's sub labels around the world. London was most eager to have Steve and the band come to the foggy city, work a few of the clubs, do a lot of PR, and sell his records.

A date was set. On the very date for departure, Steve's wife, Stephanie, took sick and was taken to the hospital. Steve wanted to cancel the tour ignoring Stephanie's plea that he continue as planned. No way. He cancelled. Luckily for cell phones, he was able to contact his musicians who were either on their way to the airport or they were already in the lounge waiting for departure.

Steve spent the next two weeks at Stephanie's bedside, even living in the adjoining room in the hospital at nights and not leaving for a minute.

Steve Tyrell looking pretty (as always) for me and Alice Harnell.

Stephanie had been suffering from cancer for a couple of years at that point. It wasn't long afterwards that Stephanie passed away in 2003. A beautiful tribute was paid her by the music community. Warner Brothers Studios donated their Steve Ross Theatre for the Memorial. Deservedly. Stephanie worked side by side with Steve as wife, mother, co-composer and advisor. All this should explain why Steve cancelled his tour to London. She was number one in his life and she was always there for him...and he was always there for her. That was his priority.

He acknowledged my existence very often, particularly when he would perform "Sunny Side of the Street" and knew I was in the audience. He would sing "and I'd be rich as Morris Diamond."

Music biz aside, Steve has always been a good friend and I'm happy to know that wherever he plays in my area, I'd get a call from his road manager, Jon Allen, telling me "there's a pair of tickets at will call for you."

PHOTO GALLERY

A summer's day in 2003 on the patio of Caffe Roma in Beverly Hills with Al Martino and Tony Martin.

On this day in May 2009, when the Pacific Pioneers Broadcasters paid honor to Andy Williams. Alice Harnell and I joined in.

The Monte Carlo Sporting club allowed us bums from L A to hang out.
L-R, *Kojak* music composer, John Cacavas; Telly Savalas; choreographer,
Walter Painter; and, of course, me.

Bill Medley and friend after I recorded him singing the theme to Pia Zadora's film "Butterfly" in 1980. Which, incidentally, was never used.

When Wink and Sandy Martindale throw a party, It's first class. L-R Charlie and Ellen O'Donnell (Ex-dj Charlie, before his passing, was the announcer for many years on *Wheel of Fortune*); MID, Al Martino, record promoter Steve Resnick, Judy Martino and Casey Kasem.

Charo has me all tied up (I'm so hard to get!!!).

My favorite recording act, Deborah Galli and her guitarist/manager, Lennie Boivin. She had a good shot in the early 80's with Mercury Records, my alma mater.

At a recent Palm Springs film fest, the loveable Della Reese.

After Dionne Warwick was through with her show in Istanbul, she hung out with me, my Turkish partner, Ahmet San, and her manager, Joe Grant.

At the international miniature golf tournament, I paired up with Shecky Greene, and we both won a prize!! L-R Frankie Randall, (it was at his home); MID and Alice Harnell, Marie and Shecky Greene and a welcomed crasher, Harpo the clown.

Hal Linden put down his clarinet to hug me. This was 2010 at Vicky's in Indian Wells while performing with the Desert Cities Jazz Band.

Not too many people knew that the late James MacArthur was a recording artist at one time. Doesn't say much for me...I was his record promoter...this was in the mid-50's. Here's Jim and his lovely wife.

Kenny Rogers and me reminiscing backstage at the Spotlight29 Casino in Coachella, March, 2011.

Your basic tourist, Shirley MacLain and I, touring the vast underground system below the streets of Istanbul.

Society of Singers prez, Jerry Sharell and I paid a visit to Natalie Cole at the Morongo Casino in Cabazon.

A warm moment with Patti Page following her performance at Chase Park, in Marina Del Rey in Santa Monica.

Ron Anton gave a reception to Ted Kennedy when he visited BMI in Los Angeles. I'm honored to have been in a photo with Senator Kennedy and also have his autograph.

Ralph (Sandler and) Young, Keely Smith, MID and Mrs. Arlene Young.

At an art exhibit in NYC. That's me refereeing a heated discussion between two fairly well-known artists—Tony Bennett and Warner Chappell Music East Coast VP, Frank Military. And you thought I ain't got class!!

The time, Dec. 31, 1944. Sgt. Morris I Diamond, U.S Air Tansport Command, Nettie Diamond, celebrating New Year's eve with Lorraine and Ken (Festus) Curtis in Hollywood.

It was not a tearful parting, but Shirley MacLaine couldn't take her hands off me saying our goodbyes in Turkey in the late 80's.

The Orphan Punks is one of Chicago's staples in rock 'n roll. Proudly, I give you my twin Grandsons, Brian Masterson (deceased, 2002); Brian Setzer; Grandson, Darrell Masterson. Kneeling, Ashley Wolfgang. The group, in tribute to my Grandson, Brian, still remain one of Chicago's hottest rock groups. Their main rule amongst themselves...no smoking or drinking.

After one of her shows in Istanbul, Liza Minnelli takes time out to be nice to me and favorite pianist, Billy Stritch.

Here I am watching Eddie Fisher make faces at my #1 client (at the time); Bruce Weil, who was waiting his turn to be interviewed for a radio show. Circa 1955.

My younger daughter, Allyn Marie Geinosky, trying to please me by wearing a Yankee Hat. What makes her think I would like that??? Because I'm wearing an original Yankee Jacket? Probably. That's my granddaughter, Helen, climbing all over both of us.

A time out in our tour of Moscow, LaToya Jackson, Elena Diamond and our hosts, Hiroshi and Nobu Kuwashima. LaToya was loved by all at her show at the Olympia Stadium.

Visiting in Chicago in 1966 was London recording artist, Julie Rogers.
I was relegated to squire her around. We popped in on one of my
favorite recording studios and bumped into Louie Armstrong.

Chapter Thirty-Five
KEELY SMITH

Here's a name that I literally dropped a number of years ago, then we discovered each other years later and we've been in like ever since. I'd say we've been in love ever since, but when we talk about the possibility of having sex with each other, we both laugh ourselves silly. We both knew it could never happen, but she did turn out to be one of my lifetime best buddies.

I didn't meet Keely until the mid '60s after she married legendary record producer, Jimmy Bowen. I recall them having a beautiful home on Kling Street in Studio City and visited with them on a number of occasions.

An incident of note occurred while working out of the Pia Zadora office in the early '80s. I befriended Herb Gronaouer, who was booking most of Pia's personal appearances. He came into my office and asked if I knew Keely well enough to ask if she would take a gig which would have been a cruise out of Shanghai and paid pretty well, and if I could lock that up for him, he can assure me that I would be accommodated on the cruise as well including first class transportation from L.A. I told him that I'll speak to her. Hey, a free trip?

I phoned Keely and explained the deal...the trip, the length of the trip, how many shows she would have to do, and, of course, the fee. She accepted. I also mentioned to her that I will probably be on that trip as well, and she thought that would be fun...as I did.

Contracts were prepared and sent to Keely for her signature. As she read through the agreement, she came across the part that tells of her accommodations on board which was a suite for her, a cabin for her accompanyist—and a cabin for me. Instead of calling Herb

Keely Smith visiting Steve Tyrell with show producer/Jazz DJ, Jim "Fitz" Fitsgerald and his wife, Wendy, after Steve's show.

or myself to complain about me being a part of her trip as mentioned in her agreement, she called the booker directly and insisted that my name be removed from the contract.

Why it made any difference I'll never know, nor did I ask her why, because when I told her initially that I would be part of the tour, she thought that would be fun. I voluntarily pulled out of the trip knowing that traveling with a hurt feeling for a week or two wouldn't be the smartest thing I can do.

Anyway, fast forward to the year 2002 when I attended the Grammy Life Achievement Awards affair at the USC Science building in downtown L.A. Sitting in front of my wife and I was Keely and her brother, Piggy Smith. She was there on behalf of Rosemary Clooney, who was to receive an award, and was too ill to attend. At the end of the evening, Keely turned to me and asked if we're gonna talk to each other again. We both laughed and hugged and have been living happily ever after.

A couple of years ago when Wink Martindale was given a star on the Hollywood Walk of Fame, Steve Tyrell asked to be introduced to Keely. I obliged and they became huge buddies.

Keely Smith and I backstage at the McCallum Theatre in Palm Desert.

I used to see Keely more often when I lived in L.A., but since I'm a fellow resident of the Desert, she in Palm Springs and me in Palm Desert, she's become a sort of a recluse and doesn't hang out as much as she used to. I do keep track of her by staying in touch with her and her daughters, Toni and LuAnn.

At age 82 and proud of it, Keely is still in great voice and hits the road quite often playing to enthusiastic audiences in New York, London, Chicago and San Francisco. We see each other backstage after attending performances of friends who play the local venues from time to time.

I'm content to settle for the hugs and kisses when we do meet, along with an "I love you" at the end of our phone call conversations. One of my good buddies in life.

Chapter Thirty-Six
LAINIE KAZAN

In my chapter on Barbra Streisand, I mention Lainie Kazan briefly at the end...but it's worth repeating...only the part that she was Barbra Streisand's understudy in *Funny Girl* on Broadway.

The orchestra pit conductor for the show was a good buddy of mine, Peter Daniels. He won the coveted assignment after having been Barbra's conductor/arranger for a number of years.

Lainie and Peter hit it off romantically during the run of the show and they both left the show for Lainie to go out on her own. She immediately picked up requests from major booking agencies and was on her way playing Vegas, TV guest appearances (26 times on the Dean Martin TV Show) and the lady from Brooklyn came into demand to work in films. Many successes, not the least of them being *My Favorite Year, My Big Fat Greek Wedding* and *Beaches* showed the world that she was very serious about her acting career.

I recall going to Las Vegas to be with them when she starred at the MGM Hotel. It was that week end that I had to tell her the bad news that Robert Kennedy had been assassinated. I waited until after her 9 p.m. show to break the news to her. She, Peter and I then went to the coffee shop for some coffee and commiserated with each other as to how we felt about the horrible news.

Lainie continued starring in her films through the years, picking up some choice roles on TV series such as *Desperate Housewives* (2010) playing the part of the producer of sexy internet clips; hiring the desperate housewives, posing as skimpy dressed maids showing the viewers how to clean their home; and, obviously making a lot of money from the "hits" she achieves which she shares generously with the various wives. A sort of a "Jewish madam," if there is such

L-R: Me, Lainie Kazan, Jerry Sharell, Music Publisher, David Rozner.

a person in reality…only in the sense that all the wives do…is actually show the viewer how to clean its home…that's all, no more.

It does bring to that TV show the humor that I feel has been lacking for many years.

We keep in touch with one another via email and I get to see (and hear) her when she comes to the desert to perform.

Chapter Thirty-Seven
MICHAEL JACKSON

In the early '90s, as the US booker for Ahmet San, a concert promoter in Istanbul, Turkey, I was finally able to lock up a date to bring Michael Jackson and his show to Turkey. It was not as difficult a task as I had thought it might be. I dealt strictly with his manager at the time, Jim Morey, a first class gentleman. The venue in Istanbul was the 55,000-seater, Inonu Stadium. The largest sports arena in Turkey.

Much pressure had been put on Jim Morey from music industry icon, Ahmet Ertiugan, the head of Atlantic Records. It seems that one of the top record producers at Atlantic Records, Arif Mardin, had a sister in Istanbul who was in the business of promoting and publicizing concerts in Turkey. Ahmet was trying to convince Jim Morey that Arif's sister could do a better job than "Morris Diamond's" people.

As it happens, I was in Jim's office talking over the details regarding the transportation of the Michael Jackson caravan entering Turkey and, ultimately, the stadium; when Ahmet Ertugan phoned to make his usual pitch again. Jim very politely told the legendary head of Atlantic that the deal was signed with "Morris Diamond" and there's no way of changing it. Made me very proud that Jim Morey didn't acquiesce to the request of someone as powerful as Ahmet Ertugan.

I had often wondered as to why Michael's rider, a document that spells out to the concert promoter the artist's needs and wants, called for an additional dressing room adjoining his, and the extra room had to be draped in a bright red material. I ultimately found out that one hour before his shows, he has a camera set up in that room for the purpose of taking pictures of himself along with

Michael Jackson and I backstage at the Inonu Soccer Stadium in Istanbul.

whatever social, political, entertainment dignitaries that might gather backstage for a photo-op.

I was standing backstage in the dressing rooms area with Bob Jones, Michael's right hand PR man and looking at the line of backstage visitors waiting to have their picture taken with Michael. Actually, it was a short line at that time, and with the insistence of Bob, I got in line with the rest of the visitors that had access to backstage. Among those on line was my very dear friend, Leyla Umar, who was the Barbara Walters of Turkey. She was a journalist and also had her own TV show, and I set her up for interviews with virtually every personality that I brought to Turkey through the years, and she was most appreciative; but so was I and my partner, Ahmet San, who appreciated her front page stories about our star performer's arrivals and their shows in Turkey.

Now it was my turn to enter the red-draped dressing room and have my picture taken with Michael. I introduced myself and told him that kiddingly, I must apologize because I was part of the organization that brought him to Turkey. He was extremely cordial and said that he was enjoying Istanbul and no need to apologize.

He asked where I was from, and I replied Sherman Oaks. He responded as I expected he would, knowing that my home was in the adjoining city of Encino, where he lived. He then asked me if I ever shopped at Gelson's supermarket in Encino, which, I knew was exactly across the street from his compound and home on Hayvenhurst Drive. I told him that I did shop there quite often and he continued with "I loved shopping there but I would go shopping after midnight when it wasn't too crowded." Our photo was taken and he thanked me for being a part of the organization that brought him to Turkey.

By the time I got back to Los Angeles, the 8x10 photo of Michael and me had arrived by mail from Bob Jones. After a couple of months I looked closely and noticed that Michael was holding a toy (see photo).

When Michael was on trial in Santa Barbara for child molesting, I tried contacting his attorney to show him the photo of Michael with the toy...the point being that there were no children backstage whatsoever, and in my opinion, it showed me Michael to be a "Man-child"...a perennial kid. The lawyer never acknowledged my letter obviously feeling that my testimony wasn't needed.

I found Michael to be shy and truly appreciative of those around him.

Chapter Thirty-Eight
BARBRA STREISAND

In the '50s and early '60s, when I was living in New York and working as a song plugger and later on, a record promoter, I had occasion to become friends with an Englishman, Peter Daniels. He was a rehearsal pianist for music publishers and was always available if we needed to record a demo of a new song. We hung out quite a bit.

I moved to Chicago in March '62 and kept track of Peter and he phoned me one day to tell me that he's been hired as Barbra Streisand's new accompanist and conductor. That thrilled me.

Some months later, I read in the Chicago Tribune that Barbra Streisand will appear at Mr. Kelly's, a popular night club on Rush Street and a big favorite hangout of us guys in the biz.

I was there opening night because I knew that Peter will be at the piano for her...and he was. Spending the week with them, not only in the club, but also a few lunches and late suppers as well, gave me the opportunity for us to know each other one-on-one. That lasted a week. They left town, but I was content. She gave me her new album and inscribed in her own inimitable way: "To Morris, are you really a Morris chair? Your fan, Barbra." Yes, I still have the album.

A few months passed and I got a call from Peter. He and Barbra were coming to Chicago to meet with Julie Styne to go over a few tunes from the upcoming Broadway show, *Funny Girl*. Peter told me as to what day they would be checking into the Ambassador East Hotel and asked if I had access to a portable phonograph to lend them for a couple of days at the hotel because Julie Styne was bringing some demos with him aside from the songs he wanted to run over with Barbra on the piano.

Barbra Streisand – the inscription reads: "For Morris, Are you a Morris Chair?," Your Fan, Barbra Streisand."

I checked with the Prez at my company, Irving Green, and he called our factory and had one brought over to the office the next day. Which was three days before Peter and company were due to arrive in the Windy City. I phoned Peter in New York and he was delighted and when they did arrive, he asked me to bring the phonograph to Barbra's suite the next day at about noon. Which I did.

Peter, Barbra and Mr. Styne were delighted with my efficiency and invited me to "hang out" while they rehearsed and also knosh on the lunch spread the hotel provided for them.

You talk about being a privileged schnook....that was me. Here I am in her suite and in the company of royalty...and listening to

Julie Styne at the piano and Barbra singing "People"…and Julie saying, "C'mon Barbra, take it down a key and it'll be more comfortable for you"…and she acquiesced.

When I left them a few hours later, I was walking on air. I had truly felt that if anything bad happened to me after that day, I couldn't care less, because I had lived. Ever get that feeling?

More months passed and I had to go into New York City on business. As always, I called Peter the first thing in the morning. He wasn't at home and I left word. An hour later, I received a call from him telling me that their show *Funny Girl* was opening in Philly that night before going to Broadway and he was in the pit as conductor. He told me to go to Penn Station and hop on a train and I'd be there in time for the show and he'll have a ticket waiting for me at will call when I get to the theatre.

I did all that. Needless to say, the show was great. As directed, I went backstage after the show. Peter told me to wait a few minutes that Barbra's changing her clothes and wanted to say hello to me.

After a few minutes, Peter and I went to her dressing room…she flung open her door and pointed and said, "See, I take it with me everywhere." And there was my Mercury Records phonograph majestically sitting on her dressing table. I was touched.

The three of us went to a nearby deli and had some Danish and coffee. They dropped me off at Penn Station for my trip back to New York. I think I got to New York a half hour before the train got there…I was riding again on cloud nine.

The time between our meeting at Mr. Kelly's in Chicago, and "rendezvous" at The Ambassador East Hotel, I had occasion to visit them at various venues in Las Vegas and Tahoe and Los Angeles. They made me feel extremely comfortable every time I was in their company.

Barbra was the hit of Broadway with *Funny Girl*; Peter Daniels fell in love with Barbra's understudy, a young gorgeous doll by the name of Lainie Kazan. They both left the show. What it did for me was gain the friendship of another person, Lainie. We've been very good friends through the years particularly since Peter passed away. Needless to say, aside from a notable singing career, Lainie's movie fame has risen to enviable heights.

Chapter Thirty-Nine
ARTIE MOGULL

In the late forties, Artie started in the music business as bandboy with Tommy Dorsey's Orchestra...a job I gave up in August, 1942 when I went in the Army Air Force. He then became a song plugger back in the '50s and '60s and had built himself up to heights in the Music Industry that was beyond his imagination, along with a number of other industry-ites who couldn't believe his phenomenal success.

He had an enviable background having been head of A & R at Capitol Records, MCA Records, Warner Brothers records and owning United Artists records, Applause Records and also running a label that was owned by Bill Cosby called Tetragrammaton Records. That was in 1968. He offered me the job of National Promotion Director. I refused because I had just signed a one year agreement with Film producer, Cubby Brocolli and the head of United Artists pictures, David Picker, to work on Cubby's only non-James Bond film, *Chitty Chitty Bang Bang*.

In his heyday, Artie was declared the discoverer of Bob Dylan who, in his early days as Robert Zimmerman worked for a record distributor in Minneapolis as a stock-room boy. Other Artie Mogull discoveries were Olivia Newton-John, Chrystal Gayle, Kenny Rogers, Billy Ray Cyrus and many more.

When Artie worked for Warner Brothers Records he had a good buddy by the name of Roy Silver, who was a personal manager. Roy called him one day and asked for $50,000 because he wanted to take his new discovery, Bill Cosby, in the studio and cut an album with him or do it live at the club he was working at in Greenwich Village. Roy had done numerous favors for Artie thru the years and

Artie said that he will pay for the cost of the recording of a live album with Bill Cosby...the rest became history.

Artie was a great story teller...often being labeled as the Baron Munchausen of the music industry. His stories were all very factual and fascinating at the same time. I can say that I think I'm proud to have been involved in a number of his escapades...mostly gambling in Vegas and London.

In late 1974, I had just shelved Beverly Hills Records, not getting paid from some of my record distributors around the country, I decided to hang up the shingle, sit back, and relax for awhile on the money I was making from licensing much of my product internationally. Artie was in between gigs at record companies and decided he was going to go into producing records and start his own music publishing empire. He hired me as his #1 man.

One of the first ideas he hit me with was to have some of the music publishers come with up-front money, take their songs to London, and produce some new artists with their material. Artie had great contacts in London, and as far as having talent available, that was the least of his problems. I was asked to go with him.

The day we arrived in London, we checked into the Inn on the Park Hotel.

Artie then immediately went to the bank and deposited the funds he brought with him to produce a few albums. As I recall, the amount was $75,000.

That evening we went to an elegant restaurant on Curzon Street for a delightful dinner. Aside from their excellent food, the eatery also boasted one of the classier casinos in town on an upper floor. It seemed as though word had gotten around that Artie just deposited a huge sum of dollars in a local bank. We were welcomed into the casino royally. We both sat down for a little blackjack. I played for awhile and was quite tired having been on the run all day since arriving in town. I begged off and went back to our two bedroom suite at the hotel for a good night's sleep.

Two hours later I was awakened by Artie...about midnight, I would guess. He wanted to tell me that one of the gals who worked at the casino was going to come by at 4 a.m. I congratulated him on getting lucky and begged to go back to sleep. At 5 a.m. he wouldn't let go. He had to tell me that she had a plan for him to come to the casino and gamble every night that he's in town and he would absolutely win. Guaranteed! And she would come to the hotel every night at 4 a.m. and retrieve half of the winnings for herself. I would be allowed to play at the same table. I told Artie that I felt it was a scam and not to do it; however, Telly Savalas, whose London flat was my home away from home for many years, was someone we should talk to. Telly knew every casino in London, having spent much time in them through the years and would know a scam if there was one. I remembered that Telly was shooting *Kojak* all week in Universal City on the New York set at Universal Studios. I phoned him and was able to reach him in his trailer between takes. Artie explained it all to him and Telly gave him the advice in two words, "Back off." That's all Artie had to hear to disregard mine and Telly's suggestions not to go through with it.

We spent all our daytimes in the recording studios and our evenings at the blackjack table. Artie was betting his usual couple of hundred pounds at five of the six places on the blackjack table. I was content with my 5 pound bets at the 6th seat. I was amazed. Artie never lost a hand and neither did I. Oh, there were a number of times when we busted…but we got paid anyway. They weren't concerned with my "winnings." At the end of the week I was pleased to buy a rather expensive Burberry trench coat with my loot.

After a few days Artie decided to call our Los Angeles attorney and have him fly over to work out some of the deals that we had made with artists and music publishers in London. He asked me to go back to Beverly Hills and "mind the store" as he would need my room in the suite for the lawyer when he arrives. That I did, but not before warning Artie to go easy at the casino. I left with an expected Artie remark, "I'll be ok."

Artie returned home and to our office a week later. I sensed that he had something to say to me, but was hesitating because it wasn't all good. I was right. It seems that the day before Artie was to leave London for home, he withdrew all of the remaining money from the local bank. He didn't notify the casino that he was leaving the next morning. Somehow they knew it.

His last night at the casino was a fiasco. They got him but good. He left London owing the casino forty-nine thousand pounds. He lost everything he won all week…and more. Oddly enough, many of us would hit our head against a wall, but with Artie, it was just another gambling event. Amazingly, he took his losses very smoothly, as he did every predicament that came upon him; and there were many.

About a month later, Artie's wife, who was our secretary, announced that there was a gentleman from London at the front door. Artie would never shirk the responsibility of facing an opponent in a "discussion" about money…or anything. Naturally, the gentleman was there to work out a deal for Artie to pay up his losses of 49,000 pounds owed to the casino. Artie later told me that the Brit was pleased to walk away with a check for $10,000 to settle the debt.

Since working with Artie, I had become quite friendly with Olivia Newton-John. She and Artie were friends before her first hit record when she was still living in London. Olivia was getting set to play the Diplomat Hotel in Hollywood, Florida. Her arranger/conductor/partner, John Farrar, would go along and while there they were going to plan her next album. Artie suggested that I fly down with them for the week and submit a couple of the songs that was in our new catalog. That was fine with me.

When I got to the airport, Olivia was already there with John and Lee Kramer. Also checking in were film producer/director, Richard Donner, who I became friendly with when he directed a couple of *Kojak* episodes; Actor Richard Harris, and Paul Newman with his daughter. We were the only occupants in the first class section.

Richard Donner asked to be introduced to Olivia, which was no problem, only because he sat next to me and Olivia and Lee were in the seats in front of us.

Paul Newman and his daughter sat across the aisle, but a few rows down. Olivia got excited on seeing Paul and asked my friend if he knew Paul. He nodded affirmatively and would introduce them after take-off. Which he did.

For most of the four-plus hours, Paul Newman stood in the aisle where we were sitting and drinking beer after beer with both Richard Donner and Richard Harris…Ok, I had a bottle also. After a few hours, the stewardess had to apologize because they ran out of beer. She saw that Paul was a bit upset about that and she volunteered that she has her own case of beer stashed away that she was taking to Florida. Paul told her that he had a few cases in baggage and if

L-R: Grace Gallico, Me, Artie Mogull, Country-Western Music Publisher, Al Gallico.

she would bring her case of beer to them, he would replace it after we landed. Which he did. And we finished that case also. Paul and his daughter were flying to Florida to go fishing in the Keys. Richard Donner was going to visit his mother. Olivia invited Richard to bring his mother to her opening at the hotel. He had to return to L.A., but we did accommodate his mother and her friend. At one of the music meetings on the beach of the hotel, Olivia and John did accept one of our songs for her album; which made the trip worthwhile.

Artie fell on bad times financially, after the death of his third wife, Kathy.

She had contracted cancer and Artie had paid all the medical bills by selling his beautiful Palm Springs compound, forcing him to end his life in a small apartment in Los Angeles with a heart attack in December 2005. He was broke.

I spoke at his memorial and mentioned the fact that I didn't believe Artie is dead, "as a matter of fact," I told the 350 attendees, "When you leave this theatre, don't be surprised to see Artie standing in the back and thanking each and every one of you for attending."

There was never anyone like an Artie Mogull before, and I doubt very much that there'll never be another Artie Mogull again.

Chapter Forty
LEYLA UMAR

One of my favorite people in Turkey was a journalist/TV personality, Leyla Umar. I would compare her as being Turkey's answer to Barbara Walters. Not only was she concerned with music and film personalities that came to Turkey, but Leyla was also at the top of the list of columnists that accompanied the President on his visits to other countries or government affairs at his home.

Leyla had her own TV show aside from being a columnist for the major newspaper in Turkey. Of course, every personality that came to Turkey for a visit or to perform, was ultimately introduced to Leyla following their press conference. So infectious was this woman that Liza Minnelli wouldn't go to a dinner or an affair unless Leyla came along...but that also happened with Shirley MacLaine and even Julio Iglesias She endeared herself to every personality that she met and interviewed...they all fell in love with her...as I did.

Leyla also enjoyed entertaining all the visiting personalities and friends on the upper terrace of her home located on the Bosphorus. Everyone was made to feel at home with her home cooked noshes and local drinks.

When I brag about my many visits to Turkey, and I do that as often as possible, and the nicest people that I met along the way, Leyla is always on the top of my list. I felt very privileged knowing that she considered me a "good friend."

One of my favoite people in the world, Turkey newspaper columnist, Leyla Umar and Me.

Chapter Forty-One
TOM JONES

I had never met Tom Jones before I booked him in Turkey. We actually met in the lounge at the airport in Los Angeles. By the time we arrived in Turkey we were all the best of friends and I was delighted at his sense of humor, having gone one-on-one with him as we exchanged jokes for most of the journey.

When I booked Tom Jones to tour Turkey for a week, the farthest thing from my mind was that I was going to make a lifelong friend out of this deal. We're going back to September 1991 when I signed Tom for a few concerts in Turkey. We started in Istanbul where we initially played and stayed at the Hilton International Hotel. We ended up in Izmir and Ephasus, the 5,000 year old amphitheatre

I never realized what a fun guy Tom is and a practical joker as well. On the flight from Los Angeles to Istanbul we were accompanied by his son/manager, Mark Woodward, Mark's wife, Donna, who served as Tom's PR gal as well, very capably handling the press at the different interview sessions, and my wife, Elena.

After the first concert in the Istanbul Hilton's convention center, Tom asked me to check and see if the hotel's Chinese restaurant was still open for us to have a light supper. It was. When we arrived at the restaurant at around midnight, there were still some patrons having their supper, along with Tom's musicians at another table. We were seated and ordered our food. In the interim, I took out my camera and snapped a couple of pictures of the band. I then asked Tom, "How about a picture?" and he obligingly replied, "Why not?" At that point I put my arm around my wife and handed the camera to Tom showing him which button to push.

Backstage at the MGM Grand in Las Vegas, my daughter, JoAnne separating me and Tom Jones.

He was flustered and laughed heartily. His son said, "Hey dad, someone finally put one over on you." It was a fun evening and so was the rest of the trip.

The Turkish music public loved Tom and he showed his appreciation by giving his all at his shows

I see Tom and a couple of the sidemen fairly often when I'm in Las Vegas when he's playing the MGM grand; or at some affair or gig in Los Angeles where he lives. We reminisce about our days in Istanbul where everyone in Tom's crew...from Tom to the musicians and lighting and sound crew, were treated royally. One of their pet perks was when my partner and I rented a tour boat for an afternoon luncheon sail on the Bosphorus, the waterway that separates Turkey and Asia. Food, drink and fresh air was the menu for the day and absorbed by all.

Every time I do visit Tom and the Band, they all want to know how soon before I can book them again in Turkey. They had a blast being there...as we all did. I'm ready!

Tom Jones and me backstage at MGM Grand Hotel.

Chapter Forty-Two
SHIRLEY MACLAINE

I booked, took and schlepped Shirley MacLaine to Turkey in August, 1992 to perform her shows in Istanbul and Izmir (Ephasus amphitheatre). I dealt with her agent from ICM, Mort Viner. I had never met Shirley before and didn't know what type of person to expect.

Shirley was already in Europe and I flew over on British Air to meet her in the first class lounge at British Airlines in Heathrow Airport in London, and then for the two of us to fly to Istanbul. Which we did. I expected to see a huge entourage escorting her to the gate, but instead, here comes Shirley, schlepping her little baggage on wheels, all by herself. That showed me she was one of us.

From the early '80s to the turn of the century, I must have booked and escorted, perhaps, thirty artists at different times to Turkey. Shirley was the most co-operative and the most fun. All she wanted to do was go sight seeing and buy gifts. One of the requirements in booking major personalities is working with a "rider" that is provided by the artist's manager or agent.

This document can be anywhere from one to ten pages indicating the wants and needs of the artist while performing in a venue. Shirley's main request was that in her dressing room, there must always be a television set that can receive the CNN news channel. Other artists request bottles of the best wine of the area, bottles of scotch or bourbon—or just plain cream soda. But we must always succeed in acquiescing to their demands. The artists do not make demands that might be far fetched and most of them are generally content with whatever is supplied.

Shirley MacLaine and I frolicking in the "health" waters in Pamukkale, Turkey on a day off from a week of concerts through-out Turkey.

After she performed her shows, we had a day off and Shirley wanted to go to a health resort, Pemulkela. This is perhaps similar to our Hot Springs resorts, in the sense that there is lot of water, small cliffs and the ground was marble, and you wade in the water and get healthy, I guess.

I hired a limo and took with us her road manager and one of the gals from my partner's office in Istanbul. It was about a three hour ride. When we arrived I offered to get her a room in a nearby motel so she could change into her bathing suit...she noticed a few "outhouse" type shacks on the sand and asked me to stand guard while she changed into her bathing suit and not worry about a room.

We spent a few hours there frolicking in the water, had a bite to eat, and started the journey back to Ephasus. I was with her in the back seat, of the limo. As she does most of the time, Shirley was reading her *Time, Newsweek* and other current event magazines. I threw what I thought was a funny line at her. She turned and gave me a look, peering over her glasses that indicated it wasn't that funny. I said, "I'm just trying to be funny." Her reply, "Try harder."

We were getting ready to leave Turkey for London. I was going to Telly Savalas' flat for a couple of days, and Shirley was gonna do some shopping. She asked what airline I was going on, and I told her British Air. She indicated that she was taking Swiss Air to Zurich to do some airport shopping for a couple of hours, and then on to London. Why don't I change my flights and keep her company. I agreed and did so. Basically, what she bought were gifts of Swiss Army knives for friends. She had already bought a bunch of jewelry in Istanbul. We continued on to London.

When we arrived in London, she told me that she arranged for a limo to pick her up and offered to take me to Telly's flat in Knightsbridge. She was staying at The Carlton Hotel just a few blocks away. That was a great idea.

When we arrived at Telly's flat, she decided she would come up with me for a few minutes to say hello to Telly and his wife, Julie. I explained to her that Telly was filming in Europe and would not be there, but that was ok with her. She wanted to come up anyway. This is 10:30 at night. Julie Savalas opened the door...her hair up in curlers and wearing an old shmata robe.

She expected me, but not Shirley MacLaine. A huge surprise. Julie's mother standing behind her and wondering who the broad is that Morris is bringing to sleep in their apartment. Her mother, having been awakened, it was then past 11 p.m., didn't recognize Shirley. We chatted for a few minutes and Shirley said her goodnights.

The next morning I was awakened at about 8 a.m. by Nettie, the nanny for the Savalas children, Ariana and Christian. She said that Ms. MacLaine was walking around the square near their house. I told her that Shirley liked to get up early and take her morning strolls...that's her exercise, she's only staying a few blocks away.

Five minutes later, a knock on the door and there's Shirley wanting to know if coffee's ready. She asked me where I was going from London. I told her New York for a few days and then home. She had to go to Norway for a couple of days, and would I take the jewelry that she bought in Istanbul with me and give it to her when I get to New York. I asked her why she couldn't take it and why should I get penalized if caught at customs...no excuse, except that she assured me that she wouldn't let me take the "rap" for it.

Actually, the amount of jewelry really didn't amount to that much...and I said ok.

She went to New York to open for Frank Sinatra at the Radio City Music Hall and insisted that I spend the entire week backstage with her and I did and it was fun. One evening while in her dressing room backstage which at that time was partly my New York office, she said I would have to leave after the show because Mia Farrow and Liza Minnelli were coming to the show and they were going to have an old fashioned gab session...probably getting the inside scoop about Woody Allen. But it was a fun week, long to be remembered.

The next time I saw Shirley was when she appeared in Las Vegas a few months later. I took my wife and mother-in-law to see her incredible show. We yakked for awhile in her backstage suite. My wife and her mother retired for the evening and Shirley and I caught the last show in the lounge, had a couple of drinks, and she kept me company while I played blackjack in the casino.

I then saw her a few months after that at her agent, Mort Viner's funeral and spent time with her, her brother Warren Beatty and his wife Annette Benning. I had never met them before but Shirley got a kick of telling them I was her personal jewelry smuggler and about our adventures in Turkey and London.

Wish she didn't spend so much time in New Mexico.

Chapter Forty-Three
IVANA TRUMP

I was asked by my Turkish concert promoter partner, Ahmet San, to see if it would be possible to try and reach Ivana Trump to come to Istanbul and be a judge on a Mr. World contest.

I couldn't believe how accessible Ivana was. I had no trouble in locating her and dealt with her directly. She was well versed in all areas of the agreement and readily agreed to make the trip to Turkey.

I arrived in Istanbul a few days before Ivana and she previously did tell me that I needn't worry about picking her up at the Attaturk Airport in Istanbul as she will make those arrangements herself. We were both staying at the same hotel and she phoned me when she arrived asking what time should she be ready for the event, which was the same evening.

I told her to meet me in the lobby at 7 p.m. and our driver will take us to the Mr. World contest, which was being televised in a Palace on the Asian side of the Bosphorus (the river that separates Turkey and Asia).

At 7 p.m. sharp she walked out of the elevator with her current beau, a Count from Italy. He also had an office in London because when I took them shopping the next day, she plunked down $5,000 to buy a small Turkish carpet for his office in London. I don't recall his name, but if I were casting a movie that called for a Count, I'd go to the ends of the earth to look for this dude. He looked like a Count but was annoyingly bossy. When we were at lunch or dinner, he would shoo away the photographers to mine and Ivana's displeasure. She didn't mind them at all and told him so in no uncertain terms.

Ivana Trump making me look good.

As they walked from the elevator, I went over and introduced myself and we went merrily on our way to go to work. In the limo, she handed me a small package which was some samplings of her jewelry line that she was pitching on TV at the time telling me that she brought that for my wife. A touch of class.

Being the celebrity judge of the contest, she was accorded a huge loud very favorable reception by the audience, and the press as well gave her front page coverage that could have been the envy of many a recording artist that I had previously brought to this enchanted land.

Our friendship continued on for quite a few years. We would see each other at lunch at The Friars Club in New York and I got a kick out of watching some music biz associates at a nearby table eyeing me with envy. Last time I saw her was at the Society of Singers gala event in Los Angeles, and rehashed our fond memories of our days in Istanbul.

A real classy lady.

Chapter Forty-Four
LIZA MINNELLI

Through her manager, Gary Labriola, I booked Liza Minnelli for a week of shows throughout Turkey in July, 1995. We played in Istanbul and then down to Izmir, about a one hour flight from Istanbul.

In Istanbul, one of Liza's concerts was set up in the parking lot at the hotel where we arranged for her to stay, the Cerigan Palace. Probably one of the most beautiful hotels in the world. Located right on the Bosphorus. The distinguished audience of 1500 was made up of the elite of Turkey including the president, prime ministers, all media personalities, etc.

The show was coming along beautifully. Liza was at her best. They loved her…Until…she related to the audience about a recent tour she made with one of her favorites, "the great" composer/performer, Charles Aznavour; and she would like to sing a medley of some of his songs, not realizing that Aznavour, a very dedicated and politically outspoken Armenian, had his own personal gripe against Turkey and their alleged onslaught of Armenians many years ago.

At the end of the medley, the silence and lack of the applause was deafening. I was sitting with her manager, Gary, and he looked at me and asked my thoughts about why the audience suddenly got cold on Liza. It didn't occur to me at the time and I told him I'd have to check it out…which I did, and was finally told the reason for the poor response.

Liza continued her show and it didn't take more than two more songs before the audience responded with their initial appreciation and once again accorded her the ovation she deserved.

Liza Minnelli and I at the Ciragan Palace hotel in Istanbul, where she performed before 1500 of the most prominent Turkish officials and residents.

Front page stories in the next morning's Turkish newspapers made a huge issue of the boo-boo. One didn't have to know how to read a Turkish newspaper...in the headlines you easily recognized the names Minnelli and Aznavour and we knew what it was about.

One great thing about my partner in Turkey, Ahmet San, is that he was a wonderful host. He would always think of something out of the ordinary that would please his visiting performers. In Liza's case, he more than pleased her when he had one of his assistants take Liza shopping to a most elegant ladies clothing store where she was treated to a couple of beautiful evening gowns—to the tune of $5,000.

Back in L.A., I had a few occasions to visit and spend time with her on her visits to the West Coast. Even at one time when I received a call from Liza asking me to join her and some friends for an evening out.

TEN YEARS LATER...

I consider myself a very fortunate person in that I had a couple of very dear friends that occupied second residences in the UK or Europe. One of them was Telly Savalas, and his large flat on Lowndes Square off Knightsbridge in London. Also in London was film and TV composer, John Cacavas, whose lovely flat was a block away from Telly's...just down the street from Harrod's great internationally famous store. Talk about location, location! It was a blast going to London a couple of times a year and having a home to stay without worrying about room rates, taxes and more taxes.

My friends from Great Neck, N Y, Doris and Jerry Katz, afforded me the same luxury when I would visit them in their beautiful high-rise apartment in Juan-les-pins, with their wrap-around terrace over-looking the Mediterranean. Juan-Les-pins was located between Nice and Cannes...closer to Cannes.

During one of my stays there, Doris Katz was hospitalized with a leg injury from a fall a few days before I arrived. Jerry and I visited her every day and Doris would insist that we don't waste time visiting her in the hospital, but go out and do some sightseeing. I selfishly agreed and finally, the next afternoon on a Friday, we drove to Cannes to bum around and have an early dinner on the Croisette (Boulevard).

Cruising down the Croisette, I noticed on the mini-mall that parted the east and west drive, the poster boards, which, during the infamous Cannes Film Festivals, usually contained ads from the film companies announcing their new product to all the attendees. Only this time, were now advertising the appearance of Liza Minnelli the next evening at the Palais.

I figured that if Liza's playing the Palais in Cannes, then she must be staying at The Majestic Hotel just across the street. We parked the car and headed for the nearest house phone in the hotel. Now it's been ten years since I had spent a week with her in Turkey, so I wasn't too sure as to what kind of reception I would get...if any.

A young man answered the phone in Liza's suite and I spent a few moments explaining my association with Liza in Turkey, that I booked her there through her manager, Gary Labriola, and coincidentally,

I was now in Cannes and thought I'd say hello to her. He excused himself and quickly returned to the phone to tell me that they are on their way to rehearsal and would be back in two hours and would I be so kind as to call then and she would talk to me then. I thanked him and promised I would call again in two hours, as ordered.

Having been to Cannes to attend the annual music industry market, perhaps thirty times in the past thirty-five years, I knew my way around and wisely chose the Brasserie restaurant on La Croisette for my dinner with my friend (and host), Jerry Katz.

Exactly two hours later, I picked up the house phone in Liza's hotel and again phoned her suite. They had just returned and the young man immediately put Liza on the phone to me. "Morris, Darling, how are you?" "What are you doing in Cannes?" "Is everything all right with you?"

I told her that I was staying with a friend in near-by Juan-Les-Pins and we had come into Cannes for dinner and I saw the posters and I just thought I'd call and say "Hello." She asked me to stay on the line and I should give her assistant my local phone number and she will organize a pair of tickets for the show for the next evening. I told her that would be nice and thanked her "goodbye." Well, I thought that this was truly lovely...she did remember me. Hmmmm!

The next morning I received a call from Liza's manager, Gary Labriola, to tell me that there will be a pair of tickets for the show that evening and also access plastic badges to allow us backstage after the show and visit for a few minutes.

After seeing Liza on TV back in the States when she married this Gest guy, I truly had no idea of what to expect of her on stage. She had put on some weight. Well, of all surprises, this was one of the best Liza Minneli shows I had every seen. Deservedly, the French loved her, and so did we. She wasn't as loose as she was ten years ago in Turkey, but she moved well and sang her butt off. There were standing ovations one after the other.

Now we go backstage. Gary received us nicely and asked us to just sit around as there were many notables backstage dropping in to say hello to Liza as well and he would come and get us and bring us into her dressing room in a few minutes. Well, it was like old times. Sitting around with us was Liza's favorite accompanist, Billy Stritch; her manager, Gary Labriaola; and a mutual friend of ours who spent much time with us in Istanbul, Mustafa. He is a concert promoter from Paris, but is Turkish; and we all had a ball in Turkey. Seemed like old times...ten years later.

Now it's time for Gary to escort us into Liza's dressing room. As we walk in, Liza loudly proclaims, "Morris, Darling, so nice to see you again." But she's saying that to the gentleman that preceded me into the dressing room. Gary quickly explained to her that "Morris is behind the gentleman that had just walked in"...she was very embarrassed using the bad lighting in the room as a cop-out.

She hugged me and started telling everyone about the great time we all had in Turkey. Of course, all was forgiven, and, all in all, it was a great visit.

She's Liza—She's a trouper...all the way!

Chapter Forty-Five
LA TOYA JACKSON

"Because she's Michael Jackson's sister" was the response from a fan at the Olympia Stadium in Moscow when I asked her why she came to La Toya Jackson's performance. This was in 1987.

For most of their lives, Michael's sisters and brothers were his performing backdrop, and La Toya was not the least of them.

To me, La Toya (and Jermaine) were the classiest of the family act. They were the smartest, the best dressers, of course, with the exception of Michael.

I believe that La Toya's biggest professional booboo was when she hooked up with her manager, Jack Gordon (see photo). Instead of going up the yellow brick road, she was led down a dark deep alley. She certainly has been blessed with the talent and looks…and the hook of being one of the Jacksons. She had everything going for her with that one exception…her manager who, after a short while…and only for a short while, became her husband.

There were numerous newspaper accounts of her being physically abused by him, including photos of her with a bruised face in newspapers and magazines.

Through her husband, I had initially booked her for a show in Cesme, Turkey, in 1987 as part of the Cesme International Music Festival. When it comes to negotiating terms with Gordon, one would think that we were going to do a show at the Royal Albert Hall in London. He would poopoo every suggested price I could offer, but when I would finally get disgusted I would tell him that for the money he was asking, I could get Elton or even Barbra so let's call the whole thing off. He would call me an hour after we parted and accept the last offer…begrudgingly.

LaToya Jackson and I in Cesme, Turkey with my partner, Sherman Heinig.

I truly believe that if she kept aware of the way he was handling her career, she would've dumped him long before. Her family, including Michael, would try to talk sense into her, but to me it seems as though Gordon had some voodoo affect on her.

Later in 1987, one of my tennis partners, Hiroshi Kuwashima, the US representative for a number of Japanese entertainment companies, told me that one of his companies in Japan was putting a show together to be performed at the Olympic Stadium in Moscow. I had known about this venue because of the many recording artists that have appeared there from time to time along with a few Eurovision Song Contests.

I mentioned a few names along with La Toya who I knew would be available for that date and within Hiroshi's budget. He thought that his clients would approve of having La Toya and asked me to go ahead and lock it up.

Surprisingly I had no opposition from Gordon and La Toya was delighted. It was a great deal for me, personally, because aside from my commission, it did include an all- expense paid first class round/trip from Los Angeles to Moscow for my wife and me, hotel included.

LaToya Jackson and me making ourselves pretty before facing the Moscow-ites.

The date was set and our traveling materials were all in order, including our visas. I gave Jack Gordon his and La Toya's flight tickets as well. We had a few weeks before the trip and he mentioned that he would take an earlier flight and see us in Moscow. That was ok with us.

We arrived in Russia and were warmly greeted by a young man who said he would be our host and guide for our days in Moscow. He was pleasant. We also found out later that he was a KGB man. That wasn't so pleasant, mainly because we were afraid to make any moves that would seem incriminating. No harm done. By the time he got to know us, he was ready to leave Russia and come to the US to live...which, by the way, he did...about a year later. He now lives in Boston. Our gain?

Getting back to the trip to Moscow a few days before the engagement, we had no idea where La Toya was. Not she nor Jack Gordon were anywhere to be seen in Moscow. They finally showed up the afternoon

LaToya Jackson and me in Hamburg, Germany.

of the day before the show, in time for rehearsal. Jack said that they had to go to Japan first. While they were at rehearsal, I took a look at their baggage tags to see, in fact, if they did come from Japan... and if not, from where? In walks Jack while I'm looking at the tags and he accused me of going through their luggage. The back and forth arguments carried on throughout the engagement. La Toya would ask Jack to back off, but he was a persistent cuss. After that trip, we never spoke to each other again. He died in 2005 at the age of 65.

La Toya's father's book, *The Jacksons* relates in part to the horrific treatment La Toya encountered with Gordon.

Through the years, La Toya has been ensconced in her Las Vegas home and had very little contact with the world until the death of Michael. It has been rumored that she will get back in the saddle and start a new recording association along with personal appearances, where she rightfully belongs.

Chapter Forty-Six
JERMAINE JACKSON

As early as 1968, the early years of The Jackson Five, Jermaine shared the lead vocals with Michael. He's since had his share of success with recording contracts with Motown, (he was married at the time to Hazel Gordy, the daughter of Berry Gordy, the owner of Motown).

History tells us that even when his siblings left Motown to take a deal with Epic Records, Jermaine stayed with Motown. He had Grammy awards and chart listings of his own all through the years. There were many reunions of The Jacksons but it was never like 'the old days' with the Jackson Five. Jermaine held his own with best selling product.

In 1985, he recorded a duet with Pia Zadora, "When The Rain Begins To Fall." A tune taken from one of Pia's films, *Voyage of the Rock Aliens*. Not one of Pia's best films, but this tune and recording by Pia and Jermaine turned out to be a monster hit in Europe.

This is where I came in. Having represented Pia since 1980, and taken the music from her previous films to MIDEM (the world-wide music market in Cannes) I was delighted at the reception this recording received.

The MIDEM brass asked me for Pia and Jermaine to perform at the annual Gala at the Palais in Cannes. Standing ovation! I was thrilled to be there and be a part of the excitement. We all flew over to MIDEM on Pia's husband's jet and that's where Jermaine and I really began to get to know each other and became buddy-buddy. A friendship that carried over through the years via luncheons and dinners.

Jermaine Jackson and me in Cannes, France.

When I started booking acts in Turkey in 1986, I was fortunate to have gotten okays from La Toya's manager, Jack Gordon; Michael's manager, Jim Morey; and from Jermaine's manager/attorney, Joel Katz. In 1987, La Toya was the first of the three to perform at the Cesme Music Festival located south of Izmir. Jermaine followed a couple of years later at the same venue; and Michael a year after; but at the 55,000 seat Inonu Stadium in Istanbul, courtesy of his manager, Jim Morey.

Jermaine Jackson and me in Cesme, Turkey for their international music festival. They didn't call me "Legs" Diamond for nothing!

Knowing La Toya and Jermaine as I did, I was emotionally bothered by Michael's passing. As much as I wanted to be present at any one of the services, I just didn't feel that this was the time to bother them, so I backed off. They were having their own problems dealing with the press and family, I'm sure.

I haven't resumed contact with either Jermaine or La Toya, but I'm confident that, hopefully, it will not be too long before we all break bread together.

Chapter Forty-Seven
JULIO IGLESIAS

Dick Alen, for years has been my favorite theatrical agent...and for years he's been with The William Morris office. We had chatted a number of times about the possibility of bringing Julio Iglesias to Turkey and we finally locked up a week of dates in Istanbul and Ephasus, which is just below Izmir.

One nice thing about working with Julio is that we didn't have to worry about his transportation. He always had his private jet on hand for travel. He always brought with him on his plane...the wine for dinner. When we went to dinner each night, he would have someone from his crew bring over a few bottles of wine that he schlepped with him from Madrid...and anything or anyone else that was along on the flight. His knack for picking out great wines was incredible.

His dates in Istanbul were well received and he seemed to enjoy working in this country. Later in the week we played the 5,000 year old amphitheatre in Ephesus. The theatre is in its original form... huge rocks surrounded the stage area and the patrons sat on the same rocks that Turks sat on over 5,000 years ago...and loved it.

At rehearsal, Julio came out of his dressing room...a customized cave, if you will, and saw the sun setting behind the amphitheatre— he stood there—clasped his hands across his chest—and claimed to one and all the greatest sight he'd ever seen in his life. He loved being there and it certainly showed in his performance.

He vowed that the following day he would like to tour the 5,000 year old grounds and ruins of Ephasus. He showed up with two of his lady friends—and about ten carloads of paparazzi. That ticked him off a little. He gathered the ladies and gentlemen of the press

Julio Iglesias making a point with my concert promoter parter in Turkey, Ahmet San, and me.

in one corner at the gate of the ruins, and made his little speech. He told them that this day is a day of rest for him, and would they please refrain from following him and his party as they toured the ruins of Ephasus—and promised that if they remain exactly where they were, he will do a mass press interview on his return from his tour. And if one person disregards his request, then there's no interview and he will go back to his hotel. Nobody moved. They all kept to themselves as requested and about two hours later, Julio kept his promise and it was a lovely successful press conference among the ruins of Ephasus.

One of our sponsors was a popular Turkish TV manufacturing company, Vestel. They threw us a beautiful luncheon and show consisting of a team of Whirling Dervish dancers. It was exciting. They tried to convince Julio to join the dancers, but he declined saying that he doesn't dance anywhere. But he showed his appreciation with a nice little "thank you" speech after the luncheon.

A few months following, back in Los Angeles, I noticed that Julio was appearing at The Greek Theatre. Dick Alen asked if I'd like to go to the show. Sure. I took my wife and it was lovely. And with our backstage access badges, we went backstage to say hello to Julio. I

Julio Iglesias taking a break from being interviewed by Albert Kroegman, host of Germany's "Bitter Umblatten" TV show. Me in the middle. Albert's TV show was Germany's version of "Rich and Famous." Photo was taken at the Sunset Marquis hotel in Hollywood.

introduced my wife to him and he replied, "This is not the same wife you had in Turkey, is it?" His sense of humor. My wife gave me a dirty look and he further explained that he was only kidding. I don't know if she believed him or not, but all went ok after the backstage visit. I think!

Julio is a very accommodating person and worked with everyone associated with our tour, whether it was at a sound check, a press conference, whatever, he was a pleasure to be on tour with.

Chapter Forty-Eight
CORKY HALE

Corky Hale is probably the most talented and underrated jazz performer of all time. Having accompanied Billie Holiday on piano when she was seventeen years old, traveling and recording with her for three years. Featured as a regular playing the harp on Liberace's television series and Freddie Martin's TV shows.

Basically, this book is about people that I've become involved in through the years. The last ten years or so, are the years that I became her "manager"...or as her husband, composer, Mike Stoller, refers to me as her chaplain. There is nothing that I did for Corky as manager that would have her doing somersaults, but I always had a ready ear for her complaints.

She would phone me and instantly I knew what I was in for when she started out with "Oy." And then followed with a conversation about anything from a leaky faucet in the guest bathroom to "there's a jazz cruise and can I get her booked on that cruise?"

In the early '50s, when I was promoting records in and around New York's radio stations...also, New Jersey, I decided to throw a house party in my Bronx apartment. I had the elite of the record industry there...I mean, I'm ready to drop a whole bunch of names...but this is Corky's page, so I'll stick to my heroine. I invited a good friend, Jaye P. Morgan. She brought Corky Hale to my party. I had never met Corky before, and she was a delightful guest and mingled nicely with the composers, disc jockeys and program directors that came to see and be seen. Corky was young and gorgeous.

Now, fast forward to the '80s and '90s and thanks to some mutual friends, we became close. At the offset of our newly found friendship,

L-R Yours truly, Mike Stoller, Corky Hale Stoller, Palm Springs Mayor Steve Pougnet, Bruce Fessier, The Desert Sun Entertainment Editor; attending Corky's Jazz show with the Desert Cities Jazz Band at Vicky's of Sante Fe in Indian Wells..

I reminded her about coming to a party at my home in The Bronx in the '50s. "Me, in the Bronx?" She continued, "Are you out of your mind?" You'd think I accused her of being in Alcatraz or Devil's Island.

Luckily, I took pictures at my little house soiree. Sure enough there's a photo of my younger daughter, Allyn, who was about one or two years old, sitting on a piano bench on Corky's lap at the upright and pecking at the keys. Before I showed Corky the evidence of her Bronx denial, I quizzed her again as to her certainty about never being in The Bronx. She stood ground and was very positive in her denial. Then I showed her the photo. "Well, J P asked me if I wanted to go to a house party with her. I didn't ask where we were going," she continued. "So how was I to know I was in the Bronx, JP drove and what do I know about the Bronx?" She carried on for quite awhile. It is now and has been for many years a standing gag between us.

I consider myself fortunate in being a confidante to Corky. I do try my damndest to give her the best advice I can when she asks me. I'm a huge fan. I "qvell" when I watch her playing a jazz piece on the piano with her head facing the ceiling and bouncing from side to side or when she's playing a jazz tune on the harp with her fingers obeying her beautifully. If you never heard jazz played on the harp, run, don't walk to her performing a jazz version of one her husband's hit tunes, "Kansas City."

Chapter Forty-Nine
PIA ZADORA

Or as I affectionately named her Pia Zadorable.

Her full maiden name was Pia Alfreda Schipani, and in a sense, was born in the proverbial trunk. Her parents were Broadway show people. Her mother, whose maiden name was Zadora, was a wardrobe mistress for shows and father was a concert violinist for many Broadway shows. Pia, as a child actress, appeared on Broadway with Tallulah Bankhead in *Midgie Purvis*, and also played "Bialke," the younger sister in the Broadway Production of *Fiddler On The Roof* in 1964 for a two year run.

After I left the Air Force in April, 1945, the first job I accepted was as song plugger for Tommy Dorsey's music publishing companies. Consequently, I became buddy-buddy with the band road manager at the time, Tino Barzie (that's another story altogether).

Early 1980's, after I had developed a bit of a reputation as a "music consultant" for films and TV, (these days now known as a "music supervisor"), I got a call from Tino, who was now Pia Zadora's manager. They were in post production on a film starring Pia, *Butterfly*, and needed some help with the music that was already in the film, but seeking additional music. I satisfied his request for music for a few of the scenes. The incredible underscore was by Ennio Morricone.

After a few visits to Tino's office, which was actually the headquarters for Pia's husband's financial activities, I was asked by her husband, super-millionaire Meshulam Riklis and also Tino to consider working out of their new offices, which would be the new penthouse on top of the building on Wilshire Boulevard and Camden that housed stock-maven Mike Milkin's financial headquarters. I salivated at the

The little girl with the big voice, Pia Zadora and me.

thought and accepted immediately. They wanted my presence in their company to be available as consultant to their future films and also Pia's upcoming recording sessions. I was also allowed to utilize the new offices and continue my independent activities of annually consulting and representing small record labels at MIDEM, the international major music industry market that takes place every

January in Cannes, France; handling Charo's independent label for international marketing; booking concerts in Turkey (1987–2000); serving on the Board of Governors of NARAS (The Recording Academy), as well as the Board of Directors of the Society of Singers. Yeah, I was busy...and loved it.

The perks were wonderful. I earned a monthly fee. When Mr. Riklis would have to fly back to his New York offices in the Trump Tower, at times, when invited, I would take the opportunity of accompanying him on his private jet. That would also apply on a number of trips to Europe and various other US cities when we were promoting Pia's albums. I truly appreciated Mr. Riklis' generosity. Because of his prominence in the financial world, he would be besieged with requests for interviews. Another worthy perk of being in their suite of offices was the introduction to Herb Gronauer, one of the more prominent booking agents, who occupied an office next to mine.

I always did and still do personally feel that Pia was and is a wonderful actress and vocalist. Perhaps, her management could have been something more desirable, but that wasn't my call. My suggestions to the "Zadora camp" often went unheeded and I was forced to witness what I felt was unnecessary spending of excessive funds such as the hiring of top record producers Jimmy Jam and Terry Lewis; Emilio Estefan and Narada Michael Walden. It isn't that these pros didn't come up with great material, it's just that after many $$$$ was spent for recording sessions, it was the decision of Pia's management to shelve the product. The material was competitive and Pia's performances were great, but management decided otherwise. I had a number of foreign record labels asking for new product from Pia, but was denied any favorable response from management. I must say that her good music albums were equally beautifully performed and did much in creating avid audiences for her live performances around the US which were ably booked by Herb Gronauer, who shared office space in the penthouse.

In one of Pia's lesser accepted films, *Voyage of the Rock Aliens* that also starred Jermaine Jackson, Pia and Jermaine performed and recorded a tune called "When The Rain Begins To Fall"; a smash hit going to number one in Europe. It didn't do as well in the States. At the MIDEM gala of 1985 in Cannes, both Pia and Jermaine were invited to perform the song which earned them both a standing ovation from the music reps from all over the world.

One of Pia's other films, *Fake Out,* was a different kind of flick. I had heard that they offered the male lead to Telly Savalas...my buddy. I called him in London and asked him if he had read the script thoroughly before agreeing to do the film. His answer to me was that he did read it and for the amount of money they offered, he didn't think he was interested in the project. He said that his agent, Jack Gilardi then went back to the producers of the film and was able to get the price for Telly upped four times the original offer. "They made me an offer I couldn't refuse." I couldn't fault him for that. Actually, it turned out to be a better than a B film.

Not all films that Pia performed were financed by her husband. In 1988, she played a beatnik in the original John Waters' *Hairspray.* In 1994 she appeared in the final scene of *Naked Gun 33-1/3 The Final Insult.* She was in a comedy sketch that had her singing in the Academy Awards scene. That was actually memorable. As a ten year old child, Pia appeared in her first film *Santa Claus Conquers the Martians,* acting and singing.

Pia is happily married to her third husband, a detective, Mike Jeffries, and as of this writing has no interest in returning to the stage, screen or records. The daughter of Pia and Meshulam Riklis, Kady, is a lovely young lady and as talented as her mother. She has appeared in a couple of films and sings up a storm.

Pia would not let you know that behind that exterior that was a little tough at times, she was a most caring person. As a small example, on many of the overnight flights on the private jet that I was privileged to go along with Pia and Rik, I would fall asleep and be slightly awakened by Pia covering me with a warm blanket before the stewardess on board would think of it.

Wrongfully, she had been the butt of many jokes, but inside that stern exterior, she's a lovely woman and a caring mother. I look for Pia to pop up again sometime soon—perhaps back on stage in Vegas where she belongs. She still looks and sounds great. A truly memorable chapter of my life.

Chapter Fifty
MESHULAM RIKLIS

At one time, Meshulam Riklis was noted as one of the richest men in America. He was born in Istanbul, Turkey and spent his younger years in Tel Aviv, moving to the United States in 1947.

As I heard it, while residing in Minneapolis and teaching Hebrew at the University, he was made aware about a major watch company in New York having some financial problems and felt that he could lead them down the right path. Through the generosity of the parents of a couple of his students, he was able to raise the funds to finance a trip to Manhattan for a few days and attend the stockholders' meeting. When he returned to Minneapolis five days later, he was president of the Gruen Watch Company.

There's no question, he has been the master of maneuvering companies via stocks and bonds. Some of the companies that he nurtured and owned were Fabergé, JJ Newberry Stores, Samsonite, the Riviera Hotel and Casino in Las Vegas, McCrory Stores; to mention but a few.

In 1980, I became involved with Meshulam during the filming of *Butterfly*, which starred his wife, Pia Zadora. Tino Barzie was Pia's manager and I had known him since we both worked for the Tommy Dorsey Organization post war...he being road manager for the band, and I working for Dorsey's Music Publishing Companies as a song plugger.

Tino phoned me to see if I can help him with some of the music cues for the film, although the brilliant score was composed by Ennio Morricone. I was able to comply favorably and was named the "music consultant" for the film (today known as a music supervisor). I was then offered the job as music consultant for the organization that included Pia's recordings and future films that were on their slate. I had not met Mr. Riklis yet, but after Tino hired me, I got a call one evening from Meshulam and he asked me to give him an idea of what I'm going to do to earn my monthly fee as consultant. I then explained to him the procedure of securing licenses for music for films as well as for her recordings and consulting on all projects. That pleased him and he simply said "Welcome." While his new offices were being built on Wilshire Boulevard in Beverly Hills, we were housed at the store/office of the Riviera Hotel across the street. I would show up there a few times a week, and on a couple of instances, he would invite me to accompany him across Wilshire Boulevard to see how the new offices are coming along. They were already built and new furniture and decor was now setting in. While there, he took a hammer, a few of the paintings worth zillions, got on a chair and asked me to advise him as to whether it was straight or not…bang a nail in the wall…and hang the very expensive paintings.

A couple of years before going on board with Meshulam, Pia and Tino, one of my great pastimes was organizing tennis tournaments for the Music Industry. Through my late friend, Music Publisher, Al Gallico, I was able to make contact with the entertainment director of the Riviera Hotel in Las Vegas, which Mr. Riklis owned, for me to hold our next Tennis Tournament there. They were delighted to have us and made us feel at home for the weekend. One of the evenings, my wife, Elena, and I decided to go to one of the restaurants in the hotel and have dinner by ourselves. I phoned the Maitre d and made the reservation.

We were standing in the entry way to the restaurant waiting for the maitre de to show us to our table. As he was handing us our menus, in walked two gentlemen. He immediately dropped us like a hot potato and went to cater the gentlemen. One of them told the maitre de to continue seating us and he'll wait his turn.

Which he did. I asked the maitre de who the gentleman was, and he replied, "My boss, Mr. Riklis."

When I finally got to meet Meshulam, I reminded him of the incident. He smiled. From then on, every time we were in someone's company, he would say to me, "Moishele, tell them the story about the restaurant and what I nice guy I am."

Meshulam Riklis baby-sitting Kady with Mommy Pia Zadora looking on. This was en route on "Rik's" jet to one of Pia' personal appearances.

I give Meshulam Riklis a high rating for Class with a capitol C. We were flying to London on his private jet for a show that Pia was to perform for the BBC. He had with him a few of his business associates and I was sitting close by the round table that was set in front of the plane. He was mentioning to them that in a couple of days, he will fly to Israel to visit his parents. After awhile I asked if he was really going to Israel. He asked if I had ever been there. I truthfully said no. We were to arrive in London on a Monday morning. He said "Be in front of our hotel Wednesday morning at ten a.m. and we'll go to Israel." I was on time. Along with Rik and his associates, we limo'd back to Heathrow on Wednesday morning and flew to Israel.

As we approached the landing at the Ben Gurion International Airport, he invited me to go up to the cockpit with the pilots and that was a thrilling experience. We were met by a couple of limos and a jeep with a few Israeli soldiers. The soldiers were there to take Rik to the hospital where his father was recovering from an illness. The remainder of us were taken to the Tel Aviv Hilton where we were already checked-in.

That evening I took my own tour to a museum in Jaffa that had a show that was all about what Israel is all about. I had a bite to eat at one of the sidewalk cafes and wended my way back to the Hilton. I went directly to the concierge and requested a tour for the next day. The gentleman asked my name and I told him. He checked his file and advised me that Mr. Riklis had already organized a driver to take me on a private tour to Jerusalem, Mt. Sinai, the great wall, and all the religious sites that everyone must see. I was flabbergasted at Rik's thoughtfulness. I couldn't wait 'till morning.

I was picked up on time and off we went. Yes, I did take a picture on a camel on top of Mt. Sinai. The driver was a wonderful guide. We took time out for lunch and he would not let me pick up the check. When he dropped me off back at the hotel, I offered him a decent tip. He thanked me and said that Mr. Riklis has taken care of everything. But to show what kind of a "mensch" Rik is, with all his buddies there and spending time to visit his parents...he took the time to make sure that I had a great time. Which I'll never forget...both the great time—and Meshulam.

While on promotion road trips for Pia's albums, the attending press would ask for an interview and his reply would always be "today I'm Mr. Zadora, the husband of the person you came to interview. Talk to her." He never wanted to take the spotlight away from his wife.

Mr. Riklis was ecstatic after I took the soundtrack of *Butterfly* to MIDEM to a acquire sub-publishing and master rights licenses for which music and master was also published by Par Par Music, our ASCAP company; and I returned home with $86,000 worth of commitments from music publishing and record companies from around the world.

I cherished the association that lasted twenty-one years. I still see Meshulam from time to time, particularly at the night club

Mr. Riklis' jet and part of the Pia Zadora working crew. L. Dick Gary, marketing; 3rd person from left, Tino Barzie, Pia's manager; next is Ben Scotti, of Scotti Brothers promotion; next is Mr. Riklis and I am at the extreme right....getting ready for a record promotion tour.

performances of his daughter, Kady, who has turned out to be a wonderful actress and sings up a storm. She has a few films under her belt and as of this writing, Kady Zadora is in a recording studio preparing her new album.

Rik gets a medal for being the most doting parent I ever met. His children came first...no matter what. That's big.

Chapter Fifty-One
JACK WARNER

When I started Beverly Hills Records, I was quite fortunate to have been associated with a number of people through the years that felt I could do a good job and possibly come up with a record company that could succeed.

One of those was George "Bullets" Durgom, a personal manager... and a character in his own right that made him a close confidant to people no less famous as Sinatra and film magnate, Jack Warner. Bullets managed personalities such as Jackie Gleason, Ilke Sommer, Merv Griffin, Burgess Meredith, Trini Lopez and a number of others during his long illustrious career.

During the years that I was band-boy/assistant manager with the Tommy Dorsey Organization, Bullets, was band-boy with the Glenn Miller Orchestra. One day Tommy decided that he wanted an "advance man." One who would go into a city a few days before the band would get there and set up radio interviews and other PR events to let the public know of our arrival and show. He hired Bullets away from Glenn Miller. The little bald one and I became fast buddies as part of my duties was to supply him with materials for his PR activities.

Years later, Bullets told his buddy Jack Warner about my little record company, Beverly Hills Records and along with Telly Savalas, they invested some $$$$ in the label. I was brought to Mr. Warners' office in Century City for the introduction and I'm sure he easily spotted my being in awe by his presence. Forget awe—I was downright nervous as his butler was shaving him in a real barber's chair...in his office

About two months after meeting Mr. Warner, I got a call from his assistant…"Mr. Diamond, Mr. Warner would like to invite you to play tennis this coming Saturday and Sunday at his home. We start to play at ten a.m., break for lunch at noon, and resume for another hour after lunch." I thanked the caller very much and told him I could come on Saturday, but not on Sunday, and that I felt very honored being asked to play tennis at Mr. Warner's home. "Well, Mr. Diamond," the assistant continued, "we will have to invite you again some other time, as Mr. Warner requires his guests to play both days…not either one." I was shot down…but good!

Three weeks later I got the same call from the same gentleman, and this time I was able to accept the invitation…gladly!

When I arrived to play tennis, I was introduced to actor Ricardo Montalban, a legendary director, Michael Curtiz and his daughter. Mr. Warner doesn't come down to play before lunch, so we played until the announcement of lunch was being served on the patio alongside the tennis court.

The butlers came out with silver servers containing food fit for a banquet at the royal palace…lobster, crab cakes, the whole enchilada… I thought I died and went to Heaven. It was a scene out of a movie.

At about the same time, Mr. Warner made his entrance…typical old style Hollywood, and breathtaking. He had his tennis clothes on under a robe and ascot. He didn't eat with us, but he sat around chatting and made us feel like we belonged. When he saw that we were just about through with our dining, he asked Mr. Montalban, Mr. Curtiz and me to join him on the court for a game.

He sided with Ricardo and left me with the director. We rallied for a few minutes and then began to play a set. That was the beginning of one of the worst nightmares of my life.

I served to Ricardo…his return was a bit far to my right, but I did manage to get my racquet on the ball for the return shot.

My shot went a bit to Mr. Warner's right and in trying to reach to get his racquet on the ball, he fell! And he just lay there on the ground. My heart was in my mouth. His knees and elbows were all scratched and bloody. One of his butlers said he was going to call the doctor, and Mr. Warner told him that his "ass would be on the street if he went near the phone."

He asked to be carried to the sofa that was courtside near the food…which we did…and suggested that we leave and that his help would assist him in getting inside the house when he felt up to making the trip.

Mr. Warner remained bedridden after that for some time, and since then I've had this sense of guilt, which, incidentally, he poo-pooed after the accident and felt it was his fault, not mine, that he made the judgment to go after the ball that made him fall.

He did pass away a few months after the incident. Coincidence or not, I still feel the guilt!

Chapter Fifty-Two
JOHN AND BONNIE CACAVAS

Film and TV composer, chef extraordinaire, author, served on the executive board of ASCAP and the Motion Picture Academy Music Branch. He's been there...done that. Not too shabby for a native of Aberdeen, South Dakota.

On one of my early trips to London in the late '60s working on the music of *Chitty Chitty Bang Bang*, I phoned Telly Savalas who was recording his first album as a singer. His fellow Greek buddy; conductor, arranger, and producer was a gent who was also running the office for Chappel Music in the UK, John Cacavas. At these recording sessions is where I had the pleasure of meeting John for the first time.

Our acquaintance resumed a couple of years later when Telly was told by CBS that he will star in a new detective series, *Kojak*. He was able to get John the job as composer/conductor for the new series. John's work on that show proved his talent for composing which opened the door wide to compose the music for numerous TV shows and films through the years.

A native of Aberdeen, South Dakota, John and his wife, Bonnie, settled in Beverly Hills and utilized their extra talent for cooking. They both have written cookbooks and John has written a couple of novels as well. I am fortunate enough to be on their family list when it comes to dinners and entertaining, particularly when the time came for various holiday events where they opened up their home and hearts for those who are in their favor. Aside from their outstanding meals, they are fun to be with. My wife, Elena, and I have been on extensive trips with them to Europe and, yes, Las Vegas. Many times we were joined by Telly and his wife. There were

John Cacavas and me dining atop the Meridian Monte Carlo Hotel with friends.

times when we wished that Telly wasn't along only because at the end of the day, after dinner, we'd be just sitting around, he would create a situation by inaugurating a discussion which would ultimately turn into a heated argument and he would walk out of the room leaving John and I screaming at each other. It was all in fun, but also very exasperating. But that was one of Telly's ideas of having fun.

Aside from scoring the music for *Kojak*, John's TV credits include *Hawaii Five-0, Mrs. Columbo, The Bionic Woman, Buck Rogers in the 25th Century* and a number of movie-of-the-week specials. His most noted feature films were Universal's *Airport '77* and *Airport '75.*

I recall in reading his latest book: *It's More Than do-re-mi: My Life In Music.* When in his teens and a fairly good sax player, he was hired by a touring all-black band. Not so much because of his ability as a reed man, but because he was the only white man in the group and he was designated as the one who would make the hotel reservations for the traveling band and then register all band members and get the keys to the rooms before the desk clerk caught on.

My hero!

Chapter Fifty-Three
EARLE HAGEN

Earle Hagen, noted composer of the music for *I Spy*, *The Danny Thomas Show*, *The Griffith Show*, *The Dick Van Dyke Show*, *Gomer Pyl*, *That Girl*, *The Mod Squad* and the great standard, *Harlem Nocturn*.

He paid his dues in laying the groundwork for his future. In the late '30s, he played trombone for Benny Goodman and Tommy Dorsey (three years before I joined TD) and was orchestrator and arranger for many 20th Century Fox films until he met ex-actor Sheldon Leonard who was to be the producer of many TV shows and hired Earle to score the music.

On a trip to Palm Springs a few years ago with my older daughter, JoAnne, we were house guests of JoAnne's friend, Audrey Sedita, the original owner of 95 Women's Workout World Gyms.

Audrey was very friendly with Earle Hagen and his wife Laura and thought it would be nice for me to meet him. She called Earle and locked up an appointment. He asked me to join him to have a nosh in Palm Desert. Within a short period of time, we found that we had much in common, in that we knew so many of the same people in the entertainment business. Particularly Sam Denoff and Bill Persky, who wrote and produced *That Girl* along with writing for many of the Dick Van Dyke shows, all of which were supplied music by Earle Hagen.

I had known Sam and Bill way back in New York City in my independent record plugging days when I spent much time at WNEW on 46th & 5th where Sam and Bill were writing copy for the radio station. They had composed a Christmas song that I publish which is a story in itself that you can read about in the Sinatra chapter of this book.

Laura and Earle Hagen with me looking on.

In subsequent meetings with Earle and his wife Laura, who, incidentally is a wonderful entertainer and handles a vocal beautifully, he had decided that he would like to make a deal for his music publishing empire to have a major music publisher either purchase his company or just have them administrate it.

He designated me to represent him and offered me a fair commission. I worked closely with Earle and his attorney, Michael Andelson.

I contacted Warner-Chappell Music Publishing, one of the top Music Publishing companies in the world. After a few meetings with them and other meetings with Earle and Michael, we had come to a deal and contracts were drawn.

Warner-Chappell Music's attorney mailed a copy of the agreement to Earle, Michael and I. When I read the first couple of paragraphs, I went livid. I couldn't believe what I read.

Obviously, in preparing the agreement, one of the assistants at Warner-Chappell blatantly copied an old form and addressed the agreements' terms, not to Earle, but to another composer who they previously signed. The secretary simply forgot to change the name to Earle's.

Needless to say, when Earle and his attorney, Michael Andelson noticed the horrendous mistake on their copy of the agreement, they immediately called me and asked me to call Warner-Chappell to cancel the deal.

Earle felt that if they could let a mistake like that happen, they could possibly be negligent as well with his music. I couldn't fault Earle or Michael with their decision, although it was a blow for me financially. Nonetheless I still kept in touch with Earle and his wife, Laura, when I'd take my side trips to Palm Springs.

In the interim, Earle made an administration deal with another publisher who he was friendly with.

I subsequently moved to the desert. Earle had not been well and most of my visits to him were at Eisenhower Medical Hospital. The last time we spoke during one of my visits, he did mention that he wasn't very pleased with the statements he was getting from his new music publisher and he would want to resume talks about me taking his publishing elsewhere when he returned home. I was elated.

However, Earle passed away May 26, 2008, two weeks after our conversation. My sadness was not the loss of a potential financial gain, but the loss of a friend, who I wish I had known for many, many years.

Laura Hagen's singing continues to please audiences at clubs in and around California.

Chapter Fifty-Four
MELISSA MANCHESTER

My high school years were at Theodore Roosevelt High in The Bronx. Two of my classmates through that high school were David and Ruthie Manchester. Dave was the bassoonist in the school orchestra. We bummed our way through high school together and were re-acquainted after the war in 1945.

We found ourselves living two blocks from each other in the West Bronx. When we met we both had two daughters...mine, JoAnne and Allyn, and their daughters, Melissa and Claudia. Our daughters became fast friends through the years. JoAnne and Claudia teamed up as did Allyn and Melissa. By this time David was an established part of the New York City Metropolitan Opera Orchestra.

We moved to Chicago when I became National Promotion Director of Mercury Records. For a number of years, the girls lost touch with each other. Before they left The Bronx, JoAnne and Claudia had been going to Walton High School together, and about that time, Melissa was getting ready to go to the Manhattan School of Music and Arts to study piano and harpsichord, and not too soon after became a staff writer for Chappell Music while attending the High School of Performing Arts in Manhattan.

The Manchesters moved to Los Angeles at about the same time I did in the early '60s. We had many opportunities to visit with each other through the years and see each other at industry affairs. Melissa's dynamic career included her getting a big break as part of Bette Midler's back-up singers, The Harlettes, and also included her stature as a hit songwriter and recording artist. I had been more in contact with Ruthie, Melissa's mother, as we both were involved in

Melissa Manchester happy that I'm about to be punched out by
Kenny Rogers' arm.

a weekly poker game. I also felt privileged being invited to Melissa's
family annual New Year's Eve party for many years that not only
brought in the New Year, but celebrated mother Ruthie Manchester's
birthday on January 1. David Manchester passed away and I was
very flattered when Melissa asked me to conduct the seven evening
memorial services at her home in Encino. In the Jewish religion, the
family usually sits Shiva. This is when family and close friends come
to pay their respects to the bereaved, who sit Shiva for seven days.

One of the closest knit families around.

Chapter Fifty-Five
KEN CURTIS

While spending my last couple of months with the Tommy Dorsey Orchestra before I was invited into the Air Force, I had the pleasure of Ken Curtis' company. Ken was a sweet kind person who had just left as vocalist with the Shep Fields Orchestra. He had heard that Frank Sinatra was leaving Dorsey to go out on his own and thought it was a good idea to try for the Dorsey job. Tommy liked Ken and asked him to travel with us so he can take over as soon as Frank left for greener pastures.

Frank had total disability leaving him with a scar on the right side of his neck; consequently, he was medically unfit for the US Army. He ultimately did his part in entertaining our soldiers worldwide.

Ken's job didn't last long because he was drafted into the service after a month or so of traveling with Tommy. In the bullpen waiting for the possibility of Ken leaving for the Army, was Dick Haymes. By that time I got nailed to go into the service and was fortunate enough to get into our Air Force. That was in August, 1942—and my birthday was on the 15th of that month. Everyone in the band, from Tommy on down to the Band boy, Frank Shaw, showered birthday gifts on me. I thought that was a nice gesture.

Through the war years, Ken Curtis and I kept in touch with each other no matter where we were stationed. After about a year or so, Ken was discharged. He sang with the Sons of the Pioneers group on radio and entertained the troops everywhere which ultimately led to a long term contract with Columbia Pictures filming "Cowboy" musicals—ala Gene Autry and Roy Rogers. Because of the shortage

Ken Curtis a few years before he became "Festus" on *Gunsmoke*.

of actors due to the war, he was signed to do a feature a month. Kept him pretty busy.

In February, 1945, I was assigned to the Airbase in Long Beach, California. That was tough to take only in the sense that now I was a flight radio operator and I, my pilot, copilot, and engineer were the first to fly the B-17 bombers as they came off the assembly line at the Boeing factory in Long Beach. They were all ground-tested, but our assignment was to take the planes and deliver them to the flight crews around the country. That wasn't as bad as us having to fly the war-weary planes that were brought back from Europe and take them to Akron, Ohio to be salvaged. So we flew the first and last flights of many of the war-planes.

In between flights, on weekends, I would take the trolley from Long Beach to Hollywood via Western Avenue, yes there was a trolley then, and spend time with Ken and his new wife, Lorraine. They couldn't do enough for me. He took me horseback riding and taught me how to ride. That was a first for me. He was an expert horseman, doing all kinds of tricks on the horse, jumping on and off and hanging sideways while the horse was going at a pretty good clip. He did most of that while shooting a film, not riding with me.

After the war, film director, John Ford, took a liking to Ken, who found himself co-starring in many of his popular films in the fifties and sixties, not the least of which was *Mr. Roberts*.

I moved out to Los Angeles in the mid '60s, and Ken and I renewed our post-war friendship. He lucked out in the late '50s by snagging the part as Festus on TV's *Gunsmoke*. That lasted for quite a few years, until he passed away in April, 1991. He had divorced Lorraine and eventually married John Ford's daughter, Barbara, who I met one evening when Ken invited me over for dinner. Ken was not well at the time, and after dinner it pleased him to have his wife, Barbara, sit and read to us. Aside from being a beautiful woman, she had an incredible talent for reading—with expressions added. An entertaining evening.

Chapter Fifty-Six
CAFFE ROMA

Our lunch bunch was a mixed-group. They were a mixture of talent, brains, brawn, bravado and plenty of dialogue that centered mainly about themselves and a huge bushel of BS. Some of the names (if I may drop a few) that we lunched with through the years were Norm Crosby, Jerry Vale, Buddy Hackett, Al Martino, Frankie Valli, Dennis Farina, Rodney Dangerfield, Shecky Greene, Lenny Gaines, Murray Drezner and Lee Lawrence. A good mixture of superstars and super-losers. Rodney had a bad habit. When he dined in a restaurant, he would make himself comfortable by unbuttoning his shirt and unzipping his fly. Couldn't care less who was sitting there or what restaurant he was dining in...breakfast, lunch, or dinner...made no difference to him. Then one day the owner, Gigi, approached Rodney and asked him to button his shirt and zip up his fly.

Rodney refused claiming he's accommodated wherever he goes and dresses as he wished. Gigi then asked him to leave and not come back to the restaurant until he decides to respect the restaurant's dress code. Rodney left and never returned.

The scene of our lunch crimes five days a week, sometimes six, was at a lovely restaurant in Beverly Hills—Caffe Roma. After twenty-five years of seeing the same faces, it came to a sudden halt when the Orsini Brothers, Gigi and Roberto, sold the restaurant to a gent by the name of Argostino, who had partnered a number of other restaurants in other cities with Robert DeNiro. The new owners were not as gracious or friendly as were the brothers. The "lunch bunch" still meet every week day at a bakery, a block away called Bailey's. It's very informal and the food is fresh and delicious...and

That's me hovering over Ralph Young (Sandler & Young) and film producer, Dick Stenta at Caffe Roma.

Actor, Lennie Gaines, Norm Crosby and me.

so much less expensive. I always join them when visiting Beverly Hills.

While still occupying tables at Caffe Roma, we were blessed with notoriety when we were written up in the *L.A. Times* by Paul Brownstein. He simply popped in one day to do a story about the famous lunch bunch.

A regular also at Caffe Roma, pre-governorship, Arnold Schwarzenegger, with a few of his buddies. This was before smoking was banned in Beverly Hills.

We didn't think we were that famous...well, not me, anyway. I had concocted a new name for our group: the ROMEOS Retired Old Men Eating Out—he printed that, crediting me, and he made us rather famous in the *L.A. Times* circulated area.

A frequent diner at the restaurant was our Governor, Arnold Schwarzenegger...long before he became an elected official. Whenever he was in L.A. back from filming, he would meet with his buddies in the patio of the restaurant and play backgammon with them freely smoking their cigars before the Beverly Hills law said no more smoking in restaurants or their patios. Even though he held the number one California office, he still patronizes the restaurant on a Friday or Saturday for lunch or if he's got an official reason to be in L.A. earlier in the week, he'll pop in then as well. It's a dead giveaway when he's at the restaurant with a number of California Highway Patrol plain clothes officers placed strategically in and around the area, plus the line-up of black SUVs in the alley behind assuring one and all that his governorship is either in the restaurant,

I'm in back of Cowboy movie star, Michael Dante to make sure he doesn't hit comedian, Norm Crosby over the head with a pizza at Caffe Roma.

the cigar shop or Giuseppe's Beauty Salon, all within a few feet from each other. The cigar shop is owned by a gent called Nazareth. If you are a customer of his, you are entitled to enter a luxury lounge in the same area where they have cigar vaults and avid cigar smokers can store their cigars and reach for them at will, smoke to their heart's content and drink espresso perfectly made by the host, Nazareth, while watch big screen TV at the same time.

Giuseppe's Beauty Saloon is owned by Giuseppe Franco. He is probably Arnold's closest buddy in Beverly Hills. Aside from running one of the most successful and famous salons, through the years, Giuseppe has served as Arnold's personal hairdresser during his motion picture career. The association still goes on with Mr. Franco making sure the guv is well groomed for all his public affairs and TV appearances. All this within a meatball throw from Caffe Roma.

Chapter Fifty-Seven
MARTIN LEEDS

On April 2, 1956, Desilu Productions was formed and documented with Lucille Ball, Desi Arnaz, Martin Leeds (Executive Vice president) and others. Martin Leeds was a young CBS lawyer when Desi and Lucille decided to form their production company and asked him to be their leader and attorney.

In the mid '60s, part of my job as National Promotion Director of Mercury Records in Chicago had me traveling west where I would often take the opportunity to visit an old New York City acquaintance, Bob Sadoff and his wife Melissa in Las Vegas. They had produced a stage presentation of *The Bawdy Adventures of Tom Jones* at a major hotel in Vegas which later became a film project at Universal. On one of my visits, they introduced me to Martin and his wife, Lola Fisher, who, at the time, was starring in a stage presentation in Vegas of *Guys and Dolls*. This was in the early '60s. She had just completed a successful run as Liza Doolittle in *My Fair Lady* in Russia.

We hit it off immediately. We all fell in love with each other which started a life long friendship that I dearly cherished. When I left Mercury Records I decided to move to California with my wife, Elena. Martin heard of my intentions and immediately offered his palatial Sunset strip estate in Beverly Hills for us to stay while we were looking for a place of our own. We lost no time in locating a lovely apartment in Hollywood.

We were in constant touch with Lola and Martin via dinners and parties and going to the beach together with his two sons from a previous marriage.

Martin Leeds and me on a cruise outside of San Francisco.

In 1967, I began a new chapter in my career by consulting for film directors and producers regarding music for their projects, starting with *Chitty Chitty Bang Bang* and low budget *The Angry Breed* films.

In 1969, Martin met with Lew Chesler of 7 Arts Productions who was interested in acquiring the old DesiLu Studios in Culver City. He had chosen Martin because of his previous experience in running DesiLu studios. Martin was asked to go into film and TV production and proceeded to get the best talent that was available to get everything under way. Martin felt comfortable enough with my past experiences in a few films to ask me to be his music maven at the studio. Of course I accepted. The perk was not only that it was a most prestigious position to be in, but also one that I felt could offer me the opportunity to show what little talent I had in that field to be worthy of his trust in me doing the job.

Before we even got into production, I was asked to set up a couple of music publishing companies, which I did. A BMI firm called "Tara Music"…named after the building on the lot that we were housed in; the other an ASCAP company called "Beverly Culver Music," because the new name for the studio was to be "Beverly Hills Studios"—located in Culver City. One doesn't have to be a brain surgeon to figure that out. Along with the music companies, we also initiated a company called "Beverly Hills Records."

I was left alone to do my thing at the studio while everyone else was doing theirs by acquiring properties and stories and ideas for films and TV. One of our execs in charge of production was Hugh O'Brien, then a retired actor but very involved in the day to day activities under the guidance of Martin Leeds.

After about six months into action, everything was progressing nicely when Lew Chesler came to the studio to chat with Martin. Mr. Chesler, for no reason at all, decided to hold off on any production for a year or so and just utilize the studio as a rental facility. Martin Leeds wanted nothing like that. He didn't put the organization together to be a real estate agent and decided to close shop. To protect me, he gave me a predated agreement which allowed me to take and own the Music Publishing companies and "Beverly Hills Records" should a situation as had occurred did happen.

Martin was a brilliant man, but stern. Many years before when he ran DesiLu studios, he did so with a big stick. He would always be on the set of the DesiLu shows, and if an actor or technician was late coming to the set after a lunch break, Martin would let him know in no certain terms that being late will not be tolerated. It was also rumored that if he had been kinder to some of the crew—and that covers the directors all the way down to the gaffers—he could have had any of the head of studio jobs in Hollywood. That never bothered Martin. He was an excellent exec, a brilliant attorney and a good friend.

There was a time after a business trip that I made to New York while in Martin's employ, he called me into his office and chewed me out in no uncertain terms for a trivial cab ride that I listed in my expense account. A half hour later I received another call from him—"How do you feel about Nate 'n Al's for lunch?" At lunch I asked him how can he yell at me and a bit later act as though nothing happened. His reply..."during office hours I'm all business...lunch breaks and out of the office, I'm you're usual Mr. Nice Guy." And he was.

As I did for many years, every January, I attended the annual music industry convention called MIDEM. This is always held in Cannes, France. I got a call while in France from Shirley Leeds, Martin's third wife, telling me that he passed away. This was January 28, 1999. Shirley asked when I would return to L.A. from Europe; which would have been two days hence. She then re-scheduled his burial at sea for two days after my arrival to L.A. so I could attend. I was truly flattered to be considered by his family to be that good a friend as to delay the funeral until my return.

Chapter Fifty-Eight
AL MARTINO

Born Alfred Cini—Al Martino is the record industry's self-made star. We're going back to 1950 and his first single, "Here In My Heart." Instead of relying on the record company he was recording for to go out and promote and market the record, Al got into his car and hit the road. Went from state to state, city to city, and single-handedly made the record a hit. The Guinness Book of World Records acknowledges that Al was the first American recording artist to get to number one on the British single charts.

Al was very big in the UK and Germany. He toured there every year at least once a year for many years. On one of his trips to Germany, he recorded an album, and for whatever reason, he wouldn't sign the agreement with the company that recorded him. Al was basically a very agreeable person, and I'm confident that his reason was of great significance for him not to deal with that company.

Al told me about it when he returned from Europe and played me a couple of cuts from the album. I loved it. I suggested that perhaps I might be able to license the album from the German company to release it in the States on my Beverly Hills Records label. Al said, "Give it a try." And I did. I contacted the company and was able to negotiate a licensing deal for his album. This was in 2004 and the title of the album is "Come Share The Wine." Got a multitude of airplay all over the US—sales were so-so.

Al Martino was an interesting celebrity in that he would spend most of his time at home between gigs by repairing. I'm talking about big time. Noticing a loose brick on the chimney at his Beverly Hills home, out comes the ladder and up goes Al with a pail of cement and wallah…fixed. When he first moved into his palatial

Al Martino and me being cornered by record promoter extraordinaire, Don Graham.

home, he decided to do some work with the driveway. Out came all the tools and bricks and there is Al Martino laboring away. His neighbor across the street was legendary actor, Edward G. Robinson, who hadn't met his new neighbors Al or his wife Judi and had no idea who they were. Mr. Robinson crossed the street and approached Judi Martino and asked her if she can send the handy-man (Al) over to his house to some work on his driveway when he's through at her home.

Judi explained to Mr. Robinson who Al was and that this was his hobby. They had a big laugh and became very close friends as well as neighbors. Al was a great cook. He loved having people over for dinner and doing all the cooking. Judi dare not go near the kitchen. She did well enough as the perfect host. I savored his lentil soup along with his spaghetti and meatballs.

Al Martino, me and DJ Casey Kasem at Wink Martindale's house party.

One day while visiting Al after a long fall from a short ladder, he took me into the kitchen to teach me how to make meatballs. I watched him—I made notes—and I still can't get the hang of it the way he did.

Al left us in October of 2009 with great memories as a performer, singer and his memorable role as Johnny Fontane in *The Godfather*. Not only a great loss for wife Judi and daughter Allison, but to those of us who got to be a part of his life.

Chapter Fifty-Nine
CURT LOWENS

When I moved to L.A., I had the pleasure of being in the company of actor Curt Lowens. An old friend of mine from New York, Mort Fleischmann, was RCA's VP of press for the west coast and invited my wife and me to a number of events…such as the Rose Bowl Parade and football game on January 1 for a few years. He always had tickets for the parade and game with seats in the stands that fronted the Elks Club in Pasadena where the NBC (RCA) cameras were located. Curt and his wife Cathy were a part of Mort's "A" list, as we were privileged to be.

Curt's career began when he moved to the United States. He was caught in the Holocaust mess but was able to escape from Poland to Germany to Holland, where as a teenager he served with the Dutch underground.

He settled in New York City and studied acting. One of his first jobs in 1951, he was cast as the SS guard in the Broadway version of *Stalag 17*. Talk about "un-type casting" (if there is such a word).

Playing that part on Broadway was a good luck omen in the sense that for many years following, most of the films that he co-starred in, he was cast as a Nazi officer. i.e.—the Sophia Loren blockbuster: *Two Women*, and *The Secret of Santa Vittoria* that starred Anthony Quinn in 1969. In Tom Hank's starrer, *Angels and Demons*, Curt was cast as one of the Cardinals who is murdered. To me, a good all-around actor.

Socially, we were very close to Curt and Cathy and we had many opportunities to enjoy each other's company.

In 1988, I produced a film in Las Vegas called *Commando Girls*…it was so bad I used to tell people that the film wasn't released…"It escaped!"

Cathy and Curt Lowens and Elena and Morris Diamond at a film industry function.

I took advantage of a couple of actor friends who would give me a day or two of their time to fill a small part in the movie. Curt was one of them. Actually, I had a fairly good budget and was able to compensate my "lead" actors a little better than scale.

The Lowenses are good friends and I can't wait to go to their next Seder.

Chapter Sixty
ARIANA SAVALAS

The only difference between Ariana Savalas and her father, Telly, is that she's not bald. Since they were born, I've been surrogate father to Ariana and her brother, Christian. As well as being surrogate husband to the wives he left behind, Mary Lynn and widow, Julie.

Ariana is no different from her father only because she has the same bunch of natural built-in talent that made Telly a superstar. She can act, sing, and dance. I'm being very laid back when I say that. She is a great talent.

A couple of years ago when she moved to L.A., I invited her to lunch at Caffe Roma. Let her get a taste of the people I hang out with. While sitting there and chatting, in walks Matt Cimber, film producer/director. I worked with Matt as his music supervisor on all of Pia Zadora's films along with a hit TV series called *The Gorgeous Ladies of Wrestling.*

I asked Matt to sit with us for a couple of minutes so he could meet Ariana. Matt had worked with Telly on one of Pia's films, *Fake Out*, and I thought he would like to meet her. After chatting for fifteen minutes, he invited her to read for a part in a film he's getting ready to shoot. It was about the Holocaust and she would be one of the young daughters in the film. She was eighteen at the time.

Ariana read for him the next day. Matt was so impressed that he set up a read for her with the casting people. They were impressed. Next step was to meet the producer of the film, Max Guefen, and he gave his blessings also.

After reading for everyone, they decided that she should play the part of Miriam, which is the title lead in the film. In acting in this

That's-a-me with Ariana Savalas. I told you she wasn't bald.

film, she played the part that ranged in age from fifteen to fifty-five years old. Nobody was more surprised than I. This gorgeous young lady was great and has done a few more films and TV series since.

Since I'm living here in the desert, I got involved in a number of projects involving music. Almost every Sunday with the exception of their touring during the summer, I drop in on a club to listen to jazz at Vicki's Restaurant and bar here in Palm Desert. The sextet is named The Desert Cities Jazz Band.

All are name musicians—i.e. TV and film star, Hal Linden and his clarinet, with an assortment of players from the Big Band era—Don Shelton who was one of the top vocal groups of his time, The Hi-Los—he sings a lot but he also shares the reed section with Linden very capably. Allen Goodman is the leader and keeps the musicians in tow with his timely drum beats.

They have a guest vocalist every week. I pitched Ariana to Allen and he used her. Thus far, Ariana has had two subsequent appearances by popular demand, the most recent one—a standing ovation and three encores. I've been to about forty shows since I'm living in the desert, and Ariana, deservedly was the first standing ovation I had witnessed at these shows other than a great jazz maven, Janis Mann.

I've known Ariana all of her life and witnessed her performing, whether it be singing or acting numerous times. I knew she was an excellent singer, but what I found out during her appearances with this jazz band is that she's a top-drawer entertainer.

Chapter Sixty-One
MILTON DeLUGG

Before there was a Steve Allen, Jack Paar, Johnny Carson and Jay Leno, there was the *Broadway Open House* starring Jerry Lester. Accordionist and music director of the show was Milton DeLugg. We're talking about 1950–51. That was the beginning of an illustrious career, particularly when he was replaced on the *Tonight Show* by Skitch Henderson which occurred after Jerry Lester left.

Films and TV game shows beckoned and for many years he was everyone's choice—particularly, game show producer Chuck Barris, who used Milton for all of his game shows as music director. In the late '70s he spent four years as the music maven for Chuck Barris' *The Gong Show*, and a bit of comedy shticks on the side.

We touched base when a record that I co-produced, "Barbara Ann" by the Regents was doing very well on the charts. I had licensed the record to Morris Levy and Roulette Records for one of his sub-labels, Gee Records. The demands by the distributors were that they were hungry for an LP by The Regents.

Morris Levy decided that the arrangements the group were using were very basic, albeit, effective. He hired Milton to "soup up" the arrangements so that they all didn't sound as though the group was singing on a street corner. Milton did a great job. The album sold big along with gaining good numbers on the charts.

I had moved to Chicago and Mercury Records and lost touch with Milton until I moved to L.A. a number of years later. I played a lot of tennis up on Beverly Glenn and the court we played on adjoined Milton's home. He would, kiddingly, holler on me every time I came to retrieve a tennis ball from his back yard.

Morris Diamond, Alice Harnell and Milton DeLugg.

He is still very involved as the Music Director of The Macy's Thanksgiving Day Parade every year as well as performing the same task for the Orange Bowl Football Game in Miami each year. As a composer of songs, he is in good shape. Nat Cole's "Orange Colored Sky" and Perry Como's "Hoop dee Doo" were just a few of his efforts. For the past thirty-some years, one of Disney's top attractions in Florida is known as the Hoop Dee Doo House. Being played numerous times daily.

We hooked up again when Miramax Films scheduled to film a Chuck Barris story, directed by George Clooney, called *Confessions of a Dangerous Mind*. This is the story "Of part of Chuck's life" where he claims he was an agent for the CIA. The book was well written by Chuck and did quite well along with the film.

I worked with Chuck and Milton on the music that was used in the film, using great rock standards including Chuck's hit composition, Freddie Canon's recording of "Palisades Park." A good album was put together that we called *Confessions of a Dangerous Singer* that I placed with Domo Records.

I make it a point to see Milton whenever I'm in Los Angeles, or he would come to Palm Desert and visit with us here. I'm happy to see that he is not available in L.A. for weeks before the Thanksgiving Day Parade, because that means he's in Manhattan still working the music for the Parade...as this is written...at the age of 92.

Chapter Sixty-Two
ROBERT DAVI

R obert Davi hollered on me when he heard I was writing a book. In his email to me, he wanted to know why I would omit the producer, director and star of the Academy Award nominated (in his dreams) film *The Dukes*. I reminded him that this film played all over the world, but only in Festivals…well, it did have a week's engagement at the Coronet Theatre in Palm Springs, where, at least one friend called to say that he went to the movie to get out of the rain…and was pleased to see my name in the credits as Music Supervisor.

Robert has had an enviable career…playing the villain, Franz Sanchez in the James Bond film, *License To Kill*, and the special agent in *Die Hard* and a multitude of other flicks.

I've known Robert for a few years and this was my first opportunity to work with and for him on his film, *The Dukes*. Not a bad film also starring Chaz Palminteri and Peter Bogdonovich…a story about a couple of over the hill "once upon a time" doo wop singers trying to make a comeback.

I had about twenty eight songs to mess with…getting the licenses and rights for the music and also for the various recordings that were used in the film. It was a tedious job trying to deal with the music publishers and record companies involved in the project. I'm happy to say that I was able to bring the music in for the film under budget. All turned out well and everyone was pleased and I was sort of okay with the fee. It was more a labor of love.

It paid off well in the sense that a few months after we put the film to bed, Robert started on another film called *Magic*, and got

L-R: jerry Sharell, Alice Harnell, me and Robert Davi.

me the job as music supervisor for the producer/director, Leo
Grillo. A different kind of film and a lot of classy music. I enjoyed
working on this film because Leo Grillo knew exactly what he
wanted in music and although it was a low budget, I was again able
to come in under budget and deliver the right licenses at the right
price. Grillo showed his appreciation by giving me a bonus.

Davi is truly a good friend in that he never forgot the favor I did
for him by working on *The Dukes* with a low-low budget and deliv-
ering what he wanted in music. He calls me constantly when there's
a music situation that he gets involved in whether it be for a film,
TV or a new album that he's recording, which, as we write, is an
album of standards...good thing Sinatra's not around for fear of his
crown. But, seriously, he's got a good feeling in his delivery.

I'm glad I'm doing this schtick on Robert. Now I don't have to look for a horse's head on my pillow.

Chapter Sixty-Three
THE GREATS OF THE 88s—
HARNELL, RANDALL,
MARX & FALCONE

I think that when Irving Berlin wrote "I Love A Piano" in 1915, he had to have had the foresight that his song would be the overall feeling of the greats on the 88s.

The list of pianists, who, through the years influenced young hopefuls is endless—i.e. in the twentieth century we had Wolfgang Amadeus Mozart; Frederic Chopin; Franz Schubert; plus many more who achieved fame as composers, but also made a buck here and there by tickling the ivories.

Even some years later, along came Scott Joplin, Duke Ellington, Count Basie, George Shearing, Fats Waller and Country Music's Jerry Lee Lewis, who could also play piano with his feet...figure that one out.

Let's not forget the comedy of Victor Borge, the style of Liberace and the genius of George Gershwin.

We now update our thoughts to this century...and part of last century as well. We had Joe Harnell. He was everywhere—as a conductor, recording artist, arranger. He brought his talents to the TV screens by scoring the music for the Incredible Hulk series along with TV's *Married, Bionic Woman, Santa Barbara* and *Homecoming.* He even came up with a hit recording on Kapp Records of his bossa nova piano version of "Fly me To The Moon" in 1963. From 1967 to '73, he was music conductor for the Mike Douglas show in Philadelphia. Joe's illustrious career brightened with his work as accompanist to Peggy Lee, Judy Garland, Maurice Chevalier and Marlene Dietrich.

Joe left his gig as music director of the Mike Douglas TV show to move to Hollywood and accept the offers for film and TV

Joe Harnell, Billboard editor, Tom Noonan and yours truly.

composing. At that particular time, my local promo man in Philly told Joe to look me up when he got to L.A., which he did. We became fast friends socially as well as music biz. This was a privileged relationship that deeply endeared me to Joe until he died in July of 2005. I'm proud to say that his widow, Alice Harnell, is the new spark in my life.

Joe and Alice attended my 80th birthday party at the Friar's Club in Beverly Hills awhile back and was asked by Producer, Clancy Grass, who was organizing a "pick-up' show for the event, at the event, if he would perform a tune. Unfortunately there was no available concert grand piano on the stage, not even a BABY grand piano...just a small electric keyboard (low budget). When Joe got up on stage, he announced that he doesn't play "sewing machines," but he did compose and sang a special song to me for the occasion and performed it live without any accompaniment. The orchestra, the Dave Pell octet, did, however, manage to get along with the "sewing machine" capably handled by the late great, Jazz Pianist, Bob Florence. We lost Bob in May 2008.

Next we have Frankie Randall. He began his piano/singing career by recording a jazz album for RCA Victor at the ripe old age of 18. The late Jilly Rizzo, discovered Frankie and hired him to hit the 88s at his new night club in mid-Manhattan called Jilly's. As everyone in the entertainment industry knew, Jilly was Frank Sinatra's right hand man, so, naturally, whenever Sinatra was in the big apple, he

Frankie Randall and I.

took time to be entertained by the other Frank...Randall. Sinatra always claimed that "Randall hit more keys than there are in the piano." Wish I would've thought of that line.

For about ten minutes, Frankie was managed by my Pia Zadora ex-associate, Tino Barzie. It wasn't a very healthy relationship. Tino recorded an album with Frankie and asked me to release it on my label, Beverly Hills Records. I explained to Tino that my distribution was not the best, but I would be happy to press the records if he would organize his own promotion and marketing teams. That never happened.

Tino Barzie died about a year or two after his turn as Frankie Randall's manager. He had possession of 2,500 Frankie Randall CDs that I had pressed and Tino stored in the garage of the Beverly Wilshire Hotel in Beverly Hills. Tino held court daily in one of the hotel restaurants, thanks to a close friend of his who was also on the managerial staff of the hotel. A few months after his passing, I went to the hotel to see if I can retrieve the CDs and give them, rightfully, to Frankie. I was advised by some of the personnel that just two weeks prior, the garage employees took all the CDs from the garage and left them on the street for anyone who would come along and take one or two.

I was hoping to please Frankie with my attempt, but, unfortunately, I didn't have an angel on my shoulder at the time. My lady, Alice Harnell and I, are enjoying the ongoing friendship we have with Frankie and his lady, Melinda Read, living in the desert.

Frankie also has a home in Las Vegas, which is a must on his itinerary of gigs along with his performances around the country.

Bill Marx is an extraordinary person. Aside from being the "darling" pianist of the desert, being asked to perform at the most prestigious events, whether they be charity or actual "paid gigs," he is always on call and available at the drop of a dollar.

The son of Harpo, Bill has made his own niche among the rich and famous; as well as the entertainment crowd of Palm Springs. I first met him when Telly Savalas and I went to the Century Plaza Hotel to visit a friend of Telly's from out of town and we settled down in one of the hotel's cabarets to watch and listen to Bill Marx and his trio. This was somewhere in the '80s. I loved Bill's style of playing and even singing—and story telling.

And story telling he does very well. He's got a few books under his belt, notably his newest, "Son of Harpo Speaks"; great inside stories about the Marx Brothers that you will not find on Google. Bill has composed and arranged music for quite a few television and film projects, along with a number of concert works.

Bill and I belong to the same lunch bunch in Palm Desert and we see each other every Thursday. Socially, Alice and I see and enjoy Bill and Barbara Marx at various and sundry affairs such as birthday parties or shows starring mutual friends. At a recent birthday party

Barbara and Bill Marx, Arlene and Ralph Young and me resting nicely on the piano. Photo by Sheri Breyer/www.PalmSpringsLife.com.

for my lady, Alice, noticing a piano in the party room of the club-house near my home, both Bill and Frankie Randall took turns at playing "Happy Birthday" for the occasion.

Most of all, it is Bill's fault that you're reading this book. He has encouraged me for the longest time to "Do it!" and was instrumental in having BearManor Media publish it. Huge Thanks, Bill.

Vinnie Falcone and I touched base during my years in the '80s working with Pia Zadora. He was her pianist/conductor for all of her shows and three of her albums. We traveled together on Pia's husband's jet along with her manager, Tino Barzie.

He did the same for Frank Sinatra, Steve Lawrence and Eydie Gorme, Andy Williams, Eddie Fisher and Tony Bennett...to mention only a few.

As a student at Syracuse University, he zeroed in on classical music as his main course—which, after graduating, made him turn to jazz, and from then on, his main goal was jazz and pop music. He obviously made the right moves.

Vinnie Falcone making me feel at home.

In 1980 Vinnie was music conductor for President Reagan's inauguration gala.

His credits throughout the years speak for themselves. We're in constant touch with each other—a friendship that I truly cherish. Deservedly, he is one of the finest pianists and accompanists of the century and wrote a book of incredible interest re his working for Frank Sinatra, "Frankly, Just Between Us."

Chapter Sixty-Four
DAVE PELL

From the late sixties until about the mid nineties, I served on the Board of Governors of the Recording Academy. In those earlier years, the Los Angeles Chapter was THE chapter. We were the ones to make the decisions along with our Board of Trustees, not the least of which were initiation of The Grammy Awards. Our esteemed president in the early seventies was jazz legend, Dave Pell. He served well and was a good leader and a good tennis partner for a lot of years.

At the end of his term as president, the board decided to honor Dave, which he so rightly deserved, with luncheon at the Sportsman's Lodge in Studio City. I was part of the committee to assure one and all that the affair would go off with no problems. And it did.

We filled the ballroom of the lodge with about three hundred elite members of the music community; recording artists, managers, agents, composers, music publishers, presidents and owners of record companies. They came in from all over the US for this most prestigious occasion.

A number of dignitaries spoke well of David; and although it wasn't really a roast, we took advantage of the occasion and were able to get in some pot shots at him as well.

What David didn't know was that earlier in the day, the members of our luncheon committee went from table to table asking everyone to rise when we announced our honoree, Dave Pell, and invite him to the podium for a few words—and—as he nears the podium—we asked that we start exiting the room, but just go as far as the rear doors, but not leave. That we did. David approached the

Creator of the Dave Pell Jazz Octet, Dave Pell and me.

microphone and was aghast. As we headed towards the doors, all we could hear was David pleading, "Please don't go—please come back—I love you all."

Of course, we all returned to our seats...why not? We didn't have our dessert yet.

Chapter Sixty-Five
WHO I SCHLEPPED WHERE THROUGH THE YEARS

SHIRLEY BASSEY . . . . ISTANBUL

SARAH BRIGHTMAN . . . . ISTANBUL

EDUARDO CAPATILLO . . . . ISTANBUL, CESME

JOSE CARRERAS . . . . TURKEY

RANDY CRAWFORD . . . . ISTANBUL

ROBERTA FLACK . . . . ISTANBUL

GLORIA GAYNOR . . . . ISTANBUL, CESME

CORKY HALE . . . . CHICAGO, PALM DESERT

VANILLA ICE . . . . ISTANBUL

JULIO IGLESIAS . . . . ISTANBUL, IZMIR,
KUSADASI

JERMAINE JACKSON . . . . ISTANBUL, CESME

LA TOYA JACKSON . . . . MOSCOW, ISTANBUL,
CESME

MICHAEL JACKSON . . . . ISTANBUL

MAGIC JOHNSON . . . . ISTANBUL

GRACE JONES . . . . ISTANBUL

TOM JONES . . . . ISTANBUL, KUSADASI

BON JOVI . . . . ISTANBUL

SHIRLEY MACLAINE . . . . ISTANBUL, KUSADASI,
PAMUKALE

MADONNA . . . . ISTANBUL

LIZA MINNELLI . . . . ISTANBUL

BRIGITTE NIELSEN . . . . ISTANBUL

DIANNA ROSS . . . . ISTANBUL

KELLY RUTHERFORD . . . . ISTANBUL, CESME

Ariana Savalas	New York, Palm Desert, Las Vegas
SNAP	Istanbul
Frankie Stallone	Istanbul, Cesme
Jackie Stallone	Istanbul, Cesme
Terri Stevens	Las Vegas, Los Angeles
Donna Summer	Istanbul
Ivana Trump	Istanbul
Tina Turner	Istanbul
Milli Vanilli	Istanbul, Cesme
Dionne Warwick	Sao Paolo, Brazil, Istanbul

Chapter Sixty-Six
A TALE OF TWO DISC JOCKEYS

Sid Torrin—professionally known in the disc jockey world as Symphony Sid, was truly a great jazz and pop DJ at WJZ in Manhattan. As soon as he opened his mouth to speak, you knew he was from Brooklyn...he had that great Brooklyn-ese accent.

I was in the studio with him when he was doing a commercial for Encyclopedia Books. His delivery of the commercial by memory ran something like this:

"Ok, you young kids out there...you want your mother and father to be proud of how much you know? You have to get a set of these Encyclopedia Books so you can learn everything there is to know about everything and get educated at the same time. For more information, write to me care of this radio station and just mention the word "books." That's "books," B-O-." He then picked up the written commercial and continued reading—"O-K-S."

For a long time, Sid had no idea why I laughed so hard. When I finally explained the reason, he had a good laugh, explaining that he never realized that he said that. "Of course I know how to spell 'books'" YEAH!

Al Collins—aka "Jazzbo." A truly legendary jazz DJ. He replaced Art Ford, the all night jock on WNEW on 46th & 5th in Manhattan.

Gabbe, Lutz, Heller and Loeb, a major independent management company, was one of my clients. Not the least of these were in their stable: The Treniers, Lawrence Welk, Liberace, just to name a few.

Dick Gabbe called me in for a meeting to tell me that Liberace was going to perform at The Madison Square Garden and did I think I could get some radio coverage by some of the disc jockeys in town. I honestly wasn't sure if I could and that I'd let him know in a day or so.

That evening I was hanging loose in Manhattan rather late and decided to pop up to WNEW and visit with Jazzbo and schmooz with him for awhile. He asked me what was new and I told him about my meeting earlier that day with Dick Gabbe and Liberace's upcoming date at The Madison Square Garden. He asked me for the date of the engagement and I told him. That was a clue to me that he had something up his sleeve.

Al "Jazzbo" Collins got on the air...and it went something like this: "Ok you cats out there...listen carefully, this message is not for you, but get your mother or aunt or grandmother close to the radio...this is for them. I want to tell you ladies that Liberace is coming to town in a couple of weeks and you shouldn't miss this special show. He'll be performing at his favorite place, the Madison SQUARE Garden"...heavy emphasis on "SQUARE."

The next morning I got a call from Dick Gabbe who happened to have heard the great plug. He was so thrilled with the pitch made by Jazzbo that he doubled my monthly fee.

When Liberace came to town for the event, he presented me with a pair of hand drawn cufflinks with my initials painted on them. He had heard about Jazzbo's plug. That made it worthwhile that an artist would show his appreciation of a good deed.

Accompanying Liberace from the West Coast was Bill Loeb; the west coast head of the Gabbe, Lutz, Heller & Loeb management office. We never met during that trip; but here we are, a little more than fifty years later—and the highlight of my moving to Palm Desert is that Bill Loeb lives but a few blocks from me and we have reinvented a brand new relationship. My only regret is that I feel that I wasted fifty years by not knowing Bill and Pinky through the past years, but am thankful that Alice and I are now in touch-big time.

While I'm having thoughts about Jazzbo, one of the most famous anecdotes regarding this brilliant mind was his final show on WNEW. He had been given his notice earlier in the day. That night he went on the air, locked the door to the studio, and played The Chordettes' record of "Mr. Sandman." That's all he played until he went off the air from midnight until the wee small hours of the morning.

He left the station and for a couple of years he gave Philadelphia and San Francisco a chance to hear his brilliancy on the air. Then back to WNEW again.

I was fortunate enough to be in the control room when he returned to the airwaves. His first words were—"Let's see—where was I?"—and played "Mr. Sandman" once more to start off his new venture with WNEW.

Chapter Sixty-Seven
JOANNE WATKINS

Joanne Watkins helped keep me alive. Well, almost. I had a good run of films to work on in the late sixties—*Chitty Chitty Bang Bang; The Angry Breed* were just a couple of them. Then I had a good run with my label, Beverly Hills Records from 1969 to 1975. I actually didn't go out of business—I just shelved it, and by doing so, I was able to license much of my product internationally through the years, thanks to a bunch of MIDEM trips.

I met Joanne through a mutual friend. She had a few films under her belt as an actress...and, as an actress, she wasn't that bad. Being the active cuss that she is, she had to get more involved...the more the better. She became a producer. Her new husband, Scott Wiseman, who was involved administratively in managing hospitals, became her partner.

Together they produced about seven films and were able to add to their activities, the role of distributor as well, which added a slate of a dozen more films in their catalog.

I served with them as their partner in JoMor Music Publishing and JoGem Music Publishing Companies. I was also their Music advisor, consultant and supervisor, and in 1993, I even earned an extra screen credit as Associate Producer on the film "Double Exposure," a story written by a good friend, Chris Cory, and which enjoyed a great ride theatrically as well as cable TV. I was able to recruit a close friend of mine, Jim McEachin to work in the film, and in turn, he brought along his co-star of the Perry Mason TV show, Bill Moses. Jim, at one time was the record promoter for the distributor that handled my Beverly Hills Records label, so I had a good "in" with him and was able to get him and Bill at a good price

L-R: Beautician Maria Gabriella Perez, film composer Paolo Rustichelli, film producer/distributor Joanne Watkins and smiling me on Ventura Boulevard.

for Joanne and Scott. I hired Paolo Rustichelli as my composer. His dad Carlo, was a highly awarded composer in Rome.

Scott was and is a great cook. Whenever there was a reason for a party or an opening, he was in the kitchen. In the early years of 2000, Joanne, Scott and their two sons packed up and went east. They wanted to get their children away from the hustle and bustle of San Fernando Valley and moved to Milford, Connecticut.

Joanne continued with her activity in film distribution while Scott, the cook, opened up his own restaurant, The Lazy Lobster, which has been enjoying much success in Milford. I take pleasure in visiting them every July 4th weekend. Needless to say, I spend my lunches and dinners at Scott's restaurant and eat my lobster rolls for lunch and a two pounder for dinner...I pig out like I'm going to the electric chair.

Joanne and Scott and the boys are family to me and have been and will remain to be an important part of my life.

Chapter Sixty-Eight
JAYE P. MORGAN

I made it a point in my earlier days of record plugging to go on the road and see the disc jockeys in the far off lands like Detroit, St. Louis and even as far as Houston. It was inevitable that I would bump into artists that were also on the road plugging their new records. We all had something in common—to make nice to the disc jockeys so they'll play our records.

A couple of artists that I saw on the road constantly were Gogi Grant and Jaye P. Morgan. Gogi swinging away with "The Wayward Wind" and Jaye P. with her hit record, "Life Is Just A Bowl of Cherries." Both of those records were absolute home runs and, needless to say, did a lot for their careers as well.

When I started my record company, Beverly Hills Records, Jaye P.'s manager, Bullets Durgom, phoned and asked if I'd like to record Jaye P. I couldn't resist the offer. At this particular time she was all over the boob tube doing interviews as well as performing. Johnny Carson loved her and she guested on the *Tonight Show* numerous times. More often than other performers.

We released a few singles and an LP and they all did fairly well in sales. My ex-cohort from Mercury Records, Alan Mink, phoned and said he heard a song that would be a "killer" for Jaye P. Leon Russell's "A Song For You" Was he ever right!

We were able to get more airplay than I anticipated. The jocks loved it and so did the public. We hit the charts and it looked like we had a monster hit on our hands and I was ready to place a pressing order for a large amount of records to be manufactured, until a got a call from Ron Alexenburg, head of promotion for Columbia Records. He called to tell me that Andy Williams covered my Jaye P. Morgan

An exciting moment at a party in my Bronx apartment. L-R: Jaye P. Morgan, Record Producer, Jack Gold, Mary Walsh and Nettie Diamond.

record with his version of "A Song For You" and they are going on a big campaign to "bring it home." I knew Ron when he repped Columbia Records as a local promo man in Chicago, when I was there heading Mercury Records' promotion team. It seems that he took pleasure in trying to torment me with this new development. I got on a plane and hit the road to try to offset their offense. Before I left I phoned Bill Drake's office. Bill was a consultant and programmer to many radio stations and was quite powerful and responsible for a number of records to become hits. When I phoned, his right hand man, Bernie Torres, he told me that Bill was in Hawaii playing golf with Andy Williams. You go figure that one out...that's a no-brainer.

My first stop on my "emergency" road trip was Cleveland. I went directly to WIXY to drop in on my friend, Chuck Dunaway, program director. Chatting in his office, he asked me the reason for the trip, and I told him that I need a goose of help on my Jaye P. Morgan record. Before I finished my sentence, he stopped me and asked me to look at a letter from Columbia Records sitting on his desk. It basically told him that they are going to buy time on his station in the fall for the opening school season...and, incidentally, reminded him about the new Andy Williams record. One doesn't have to read between the lines...it was all spelled out that Columbia was going all out to get the Andy Williams record played. Chuck said that the letter came to his boss who told me to "take care of things."

Needless to say, I felt defeated. They were successful in getting their record played, but never hit the charts and sold very little. My record could have possibly gone to number one and be a huge seller.

We even had an extra push from Johnny Carson. Jaye P. Morgan is the only singer that would be allowed to perform the same song on three different appearances. To add more grey hairs to the situation, on one of Jaye P.'s last performances, Carson began to ridicule Beverly Hills Records with Johnny talking about how the records we make are all manufactured in a garage and a couple of not-nice remarks about the activity of my label.

I sued him. There was no court action—it never got that far. What we did get was an on the air retraction from Carson where he's shown holding up her album, and reading the retraction that NBC attorneys told him to read which was pasted on the other side of Jaye P.'s LP. It was of some consolation, but it wasn't easy losing a hit record.

Chapter Sixty-Nine
IRVING GREEN

In 1962, the dynamic Dutch electronics company, Philips, acquired Irving Green's Mercury Records. Philips and Deutsche Grammophon were part of the Phonogram Records joint venture, which ultimately became Polygram.

Lou Simon was Mercury's record distributor in Cincinnati and he was brought to Chicago to form a staff for Philips, working in conjunction with the Mercury Records brass. I was brought to Chicago as Philips National Record Promotion Director. It wasn't easy leaving The Bronx, but it was a step in the right direction.

Through the years I had heard so much about Irving Green and his power, especially with the jukebox industry. But his welcome was warm and I felt at home immediately. A few of my first assignments were Dusty Springfield and also The Springfields, Dusty's brothers. We did quite well. We had thirty-three distributors; consequently, I had thirty-three record promoters in those markets that reported to me. In turn I had to report to Lou Simon, who reported to Exec VP, Irwin Steinberg, who reported to Mr. Green.

After being there for two weeks, I'm now asked to attend my first board meeting. All the brass and heads of departments were in attendance. Even though I was warmly welcomed, I still felt very queasy about sitting there with all the strangers and having to try and make an impression on them.

A welcome speech by Irving Green and then right down to business. "We have a new Horst Jankowski record coming out—Diamond, where do you see it going on radio?" I thought for a moment and told him that I would go up to Milwaukee and start with station WEZY, and that Milwaukee could be a good starting point for a

Quincy Jones pointing a finger at Irving Green, the subject of a West Coast TV and film Academy luncheon honoring him. I'm peering over their shoulders.

Jankowski record. I was amazed when he countered with "Is there any reason you wouldn't go to WOKY with that record?" He felt that we would reach a larger audience getting airplay on that station. Who am I to argue with the big boss, but I was amazed at his knowledge of airplay and radio stations in various areas of our country.

Now he's addressing the art department. They're going back and forth on the size and shading of the print on the cover of the new Smothers Brothers album against the print in the liner notes on the back cover. This went on with every department...our publicist and Irving were now discussing the whys and why nots of music trades and public newspapers. I was in awe as to how Mr. Green was so technically knowledgeable about every facet of his company

About six months after I was brought in by the Philips brass, I was asked to add the job as National Promotion Director at Mercury Records. They replaced me at Philips by another of our local distributor promotion men.

I was in such awe of Irving Green. Here's the owner and president of a record company that's aware of what is needed to make it run. It is also common knowledge that he was the first head of a record company to break color barriers and make legendary Quincy Jones an executive of his Mercury Records.

I was happy to be a part of the honorarium given to Irving Green by the Pacific Southwest Region of the National Academy of Television and Arts and Sciences. He was inducted into their Gold Circle in 2006 and died shortly after.

Chapter Seventy
DICK CLARK

In the mid and late '50s, when we would go to Philadelphia to promote our records, one of the stops would be WFIL radio and visit with the disc jockeys and give them our newly released discs.

We paid little attention to one DJ, Dick Clark. As we passed his phone-booth type studio that he broadcast from, he would stick his neck out and ask if we had an extra record for him to listen to and program for his show. We always obliged.

Dick had been at the station since 1952, having just graduated from Syracuse University, where, as a student, had radio jobs in Syracuse and Utica, N. Y.

In July, 1956, through a quirk of fate, Dick was asked to take over the reigns of the then existing Bob Horn Bandstand TV show, which aired on WFIL's affiliated TV station. Bob Horn lost the show due to "misconduct" with a few of the fans. You figure it out! In August, 1957, ABC-TV picked up the show with Dick as host for national airing, renamed the show *American Bandstand*, and the rest is history.

A record company could be assured that steady air-play on Bandstand would be responsible for a huge rise in record sales and additional airplay by DJ's all over the country. Consequently, we would trek to Philly every Tuesday when Dick would hold court with us record promoters after his show, listen to our pitch as to where the record is selling or where it was getting a significant amount of airplay to warrant his adding it to his playlist He would carefully audition your product while we sat in his office.

Before boarding a flight for Dick Clark's first rock 'n roll show in Miami, Dick is huddling with Bandstand producer Tony Mammarella, and Mrs. Clark (1959), I'm at extreme right with a young lad who won a free trip with us to Miami via a contest I ran on a local radio station. Dick saw me schlepping the kid and he said, "The kid won and you lost." Was he ever right!!!

I already wrote about Anita Bryant/Dick Clark in chapter 28.

At Carlton, we also had a new artist from Detroit, Jack Scott. It wasn't a bad rock 'n roll record at all, but we had trouble deciding which side to work on. We ultimately decided on a tune about prison. I don't recall the exact title. I brought the record to Dick's attention and got a very emphatic "No."

L-R: Record promoter, Red Schartz, Dick Clark, DJ Jack Lacy and me at a party at Martoni's Restaurant welcoming Jack Lacy to Los Angeles radio.

A number of weeks flew by and I started getting reports from my field promotion reps that the flip side of Jack's record, "My True Love" is getting much airplay. Well, that was the answer I was looking for as to which side of Jack's record I should work on.

I went back to visit Dick and made my pitch. He was beside himself and he hollered on me saying "Just because I won't play one side of your record, now you think I'm gonna play the other side?" I showed him the reports from my promotion team, and as it was, that week we showed up on the Cashbox best-selling chart. He calmed down and listened to "My True Love" and said, "Ok, you win," and began programming it the very next day on the TV show.

Shortly after that, Dick Clark had his first live rock 'n roll show in Miami Beach. He requested both Anita and Jack. He asked for their appearance again a few months later at his first rock 'n roll show in Los Angeles at the Hollywood Bowl.

Carlton Records' Southwestern regional rep was Leland Rogers. He was always hocking us to pick up a master recorded by his kid brother, Kenneth, who was getting some moderate airplay in his home city, Houston. The boss said ok and we were able to get enough action on it for me to convince Dick Clark for a live performance on *American Bandstand*. Kenny Rogers still credits me with the beginning of his illustrious career. Rightfully!

Dick and Kari Clark (forever).

In 1961 I co-produced a record by The Regents. I was also co-publisher of their hit song, "Barbara Ann" and had no trouble getting them a couple of shots on American Bandstand. The song was covered by The Beach Boys in 1965 and became a number one hit for them...and me.

I just happened to recall an incident that occurred in the late '50s. A huge payola scandal ran amuck through the record industry. I had a novelty record—*The Purple People Eater*—that I took to Philly and played it for Dick. He hated it. I didn't really have much faith in his jumping up and down when he heard it. I went back to The Bronx after dinner with him that night.

A few weeks later there was a massive vinyl crunch throughout the record industry. Pressing plants were short of vinyl and were being selective in the jobs they were accepting. Dick owned a pressing plant in Philly. I called him and told him of my need for a fast 5,000 pressings on the disc that he hated. Dick replied with, "Do you think that because I would press your records that would give me reason to play it on my show?—No way," he added. I told him that he was wrong. At that point I told him that it was more important for me to satisfy my distributors with product rather than have a plug or two on the record.

Getting back to the payola situation, I had read that a number of disc jockeys and program directors were being summoned by the Payola Committee in Washington to testify about their involvement—if any. Dick was one of the more prominent of those called.

I phoned him and offered to testify in his defense because, under oath, I would say that I asked him to press records for me and was not using that as a reason for him to play that record. Dick thanked me for my thoughts and told me not to worry. He was going to be OK. And he was.

I've been in Dick Clark's company with his wife, Kari, a number of times through the years. We have fun chatting about the "old times" and he credits me with my help during his Bandstand years, which, I, of course replied that it was he that made me look good.

Chapter Seventy-One
CHUCK BARRIS

In the early days of Dick Clark's taking over the reins of *American Bandstand* from Bob Horne in Philly, Chuck Barris was the show's standard and practices person employed by ABC TV in New York City. As a record plugger, I traveled to Philadelphia weekly to pay homage to Dick Clark. More often than not, I'd get a call from Chuck to hitch a ride with me—or—in case of bad weather, we'd take the hour and a half train ride together from Penn Station. Tuesday was the day we would pitch our records to Dick for possible addition to his daily playlist.

We always kept in touch during the years. I had no reason to contact Chuck or bug him while he was building a phenomenal career producing such hit shows as *Dating Game* and *Newlywed Game* along with hosting the *Gong Show* in 1976. My contact for the *Gong Show* was always Milton DeLugg, the music conductor/arranger for the show.

Chuck wrote an "unauthorized autobiography" titled *Confessions of a Dangerous Mind* about his days as a CIA hit man with 100 kills to his credit—his claims have never been proven or disproven. In 2002, George Clooney picked up on the book and decided to make it into a movie. It was finally produced by Miramax Films. Chuck and Milton DeLugg put together a soundtrack of standards, which, of course, included Freddie Cannon's top ten hit, "Palisades Park," which was written by Chuck. I got a call from Miramax's head of music, Randy Spendlove, who was not having luck placing the soundtrack and could I be of some help.

To me it was a labor of love because I was once again in touch with Milton and Chuck. I was able to place the soundtrack with an

Chuck Barris and me at one of his book signings.

independent label, Domo Records, to everyone's satisfaction. The label had great connections world-wide, particularly in Japan.

The film made a lot of noise, but wasn't Academy Award nominating material, despite the cast of characters that were involved, not the least of whom was George Clooney. Consequently, the soundtrack, likewise, didn't set the world on fire. Nonetheless, Chuck Barris and Milton DeLugg were both satisfied and content with the overall outcome...which raised the bar a little higher than it was during the *Gong Show* days.

Chapter Seventy-Two
VIC MIZZY

M y relationship with Vic Mizzy was pretty much of a whirlwind romance. No, we were never really in love with each other…we were good friends. As a young songwriter, he hung around with us song pluggers in and around the music Mecca of the industry, The Brill Building at 1619 Broadway. He had a great sense of humor which endeared him to us and welcomed his presence.

Very early in his career, while still a young struggling composer, he married radio singer, Mary Small, then known as the little girl with a big voice. They had two daughters, Patty and Lynn. One of Vic's big heart breaks in his life was when Patty passed away in 1995. Patty and my daughter Allyn became fast friends and timed their vacations so they could meet at their respective parent's homes in Southern California. Patty coming from L.A. and Allyn from Chicago.

Vic began his career in the 1930s composing pop songs that made the charts in the '40s and '50s. Not the least of them was "My Dreams Are Getting Better All The Time," "The Jones Boy," "The Whole World Is Singing My Song," plus many, many more. That ultimately led him to compose for films and TV.

He utilized his sense of humor in his composing for five of the Don Knotts films and a slew of others—on TV, most notably are *The Addams Family* with his finger-snapping, which theme can be heard on almost every sporting event and *Green Acres* whose ultra-melodic them was sung by anyone who owned a TV set at the time.

Through the years we would meet from time to time at Caffe Roma in Beverly Hills and rehash our New York City days and thankful for the success we both had achieved in our own individual fields of music.

In 2000, Vic was returning home from a weekend in Las Vegas. On the flight, he was seated between two women. Vic being the bon-vivant that he was, started the conversation by introducing himself. The women introduced themselves—one of them was Shirley Leeds, the widow of Martin Leeds, who at one time, was the head of Desi Lu productions—and Martin was one of my best friends for years. Shirley asked Vic what he did for a living...and Vic replied that he was a film and TV composer and very involved in scoring and conducting. Shirley asked if he knew Morris Diamond. Vic got very excited, "Moishe?—We go back 100 years when we were both young in the music industry." Shirley flipped. Make a long story short, they got married in 2001. Knowing both personalities, I spent much time apologizing to both because the mere mention of my name started this union. We spent a lot of good years socializing with each other.

Vic was very fortunate in the sense that most all of the composing deals that he made for films and TV were such, that he was able to retain the music publishing rights to all his works along with his composing rights. I had heard through the grapevine that he was considering selling his music publishing companies, but keep his royalties as a composer from ASCAP.

We set up a lunch date to talk about it. He said that he was toying with idea of selling his companies and did have a couple of offers. He had mentioned that our mutual friend, publisher Al Gallico, had a good offer from a major music publisher for his works. It was in the neighborhood of $2,800,000. I asked why he didn't sell and Vic's reply was that he thought he could get a better price.

I told Vic that I think I could better the price, and would like to work on the project and give it a try. He said ok. I was up at his home in Bel Air the next morning to look at all his ASCAP statements and other earnings. He led me to his attic, which actually was a crawl space in his attic, where he had shopping bags full of paper-work. I actually had to crawl on my hands and knees and one hand holding a handkerchief over my mouth and the other hand, trying to retrieve the paperwork that would be essential to my making a determination as to the value of his companies.

I made numerous trips to the attic, accumulated all the statements from ASCAP and other income companies, assembled everything, took them home and worked quite hard on putting together a prospectus of the entire project. This took weeks of hard work.

Now it was time to find a major music publisher that might be interested in buying Vic's companies. I spoke to a few people, but I wasn't content with their response until I chatted with Chuck Kaye, the head of DreamWorks Music Publishing Companies.

Chuck was very interested and after going through all the paperwork that I had prepared, came up with an offer that was better than any offer Vic received previously, but, not enough to please Vic. I had numerous lunches with Chuck trying to figure how to come up with a number to please Vic, and even took Vic to one of our lunches.

Then I got the call I was hoping for. It was Chuck Kaye calling to tell me that he spoke with his people and they really want this company and to forget about the figures and all that's involved "We'll buy Vic's publishing companies for $5,000,000." I flipped.

How could Vic turn down this offer, I thought. Well, he did. His answer was, "I think I'll just leave everything to my daughter Lynn." I tried to reason with him that in a short period of time, his music will become public domain and lose much value. He just didn't want to listen to reason and that lost me a commission that would have been a small fortune.

About six months after, Vic called me and asked if he could have all my paperwork with facts and figures that I worked on for a year. That did upset me quite a bit. I told him that with all the work that I put into the project, he would have to pay me $50,000 for my files. Which he declined.

I was very cordial with Vic from then on, but it wasn't a buddy-buddy situation as it had been for many years. I have since met with his daughter Lynn a couple of times but, more social than business following his death in 2009 at the age of ninety-three. A huge loss.

Chapter Seventy-Three
PAUL ANKA

I had met Paul Anka many years ago when he was televising a musical variety TV series in Vancouver, that was produced by a dear friend, Clancy Grass. Clancy was looking for The Smothers Brothers to come to Canada as guests on the show. He knew that I was close to both Tom and Dick and asked if I could organize that booking. It was no problem. The date was agreeable by all. I flew up to San Francisco, where I met Tom and Dick and we flew to Vancouver together and had a delightful few days there. Paul was a wonderful host and made us all comfortable.

Now we cut to the chase and about 20 years later and I'm booking shows in Turkey. I got a call from the rep of one of the major banks in Turkey that I had dealt with a couple of times. He was interested in sponsoring a Paul Anka concert in Istanbul. I locked that deal up in no time at all, dealing directly with Paul.

Now, Paul has a dear friend and devoted fan in Turkey. His name was Sakip Sabanci. He was president of AK Bank. A total of about 600 banks all over Turkey. He would fly all over the world to be with Paul.

Shortly after contracts were signed, Paul calls his dear friend to tell him that he'll be coming to Istanbul. That, of course, elated Sakip. Now, Sakip goes and calls the bank that I'm dealing with; who is one of his competitors, and tells my guy that Paul should be put up in a certain hotel and telling him what restaurants he should take him to, etc etc etc.

That of course angered my bank sponsor. He called me and cancelled the booking. He didn't want a competitor telling him how to run his business...and he was right. I couldn't fault him for the cancellation. I lost a hefty commission, but I had no choice.

I phoned Paul to tell him. To say he wasn't happy woul be a huge understatement. He was going to sue me and the sponsor for breach of contract, but I'm sure after talking it over with his attorney, he was advised to back off.

Sakip Sabanci was in that kind of ballpark where he entertained royalty at his home...President Roosevelt, Queen Elizabeth, etc., etc. I got along well with him. As a matter of fact I'm proud to be the possessor of one of his fourteen books that he wrote...and autographed to me.

I've had occasion to be in Paul's company through the years and I feel that the past has been forgotten. I did enjoy dealing with his staff—which changed rather rapidly. I found it interesting to speak to a different secretary almost every time I called.

Tom Jones was appearing at the House of Blues on Sunset and I was invited to the show. I took along Shauna Krikorian, who for a long time was Steve Tyrell's assistant, and was now working for Paul Anka. We saw the show and went backstage to visit with Tom. I introduced her to Tom and added that she now works for Paul Anka. Tom looked at his watch and remarked "For how much longer." Everyone knew.

finis

INDEX

CPSIA information can be obtained at www.ICGtesting.com
Printed in the USA
BVOW011646040313

314667BV00007B/64/P